LACE

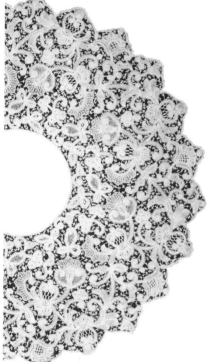

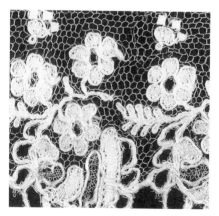

LACE

*A guide to identification of old lace types
and techniques*

Heather Toomer

Photographs by Cynthia Voysey

B. T. Batsford Ltd · London

ISBN 0 7134 5701 5

Phototypeset by Keyspools Limited,
Golborne, Lancashire
Printed in Great Britain by
Butler and Tanner, Frome, Somerset
for the publishers
B. T. Batsford Limited
4 Fitzhardinge Street
London W1H 0AH

Line drawings by Graham Searle
Map drawn by Graham Searle

CONTENTS

ACKNOWLEDGEMENTS

All who have studied lace in recent years are indebted to Miss Santina Levey, formerly keeper of textiles at the Victoria and Albert Museum, London. Like many another, I have presented her with problem pieces of widely differing quality, technique and date over many years and have always benefited from her patient elucidation of their origins. Her book, *Lace: A History* has been an invaluable reference source during the writing of this work. As far as possible, I have used it and Miss Levey's guidance in the dating and identification of the pieces I have illustrated but any errors are entirely my own.

I am also grateful to Kathleen Tipping and Valerie Cliffe for the generous loan of their lace for the photographs in plates 5, 53, 78 and 120; to Lorraine Coram for permission to reproduce the Honiton Lace in Plate 4; and for permission to reproduce the point de France flounce in plates 21 and 22.

Last, but not least, thanks are due to my husband for his advice and editing of the work in its early stages and to Richard Davin for his helpful comments on the finished text which enabled some of the inevitable *faux pas* to be corrected.

INTRODUCTION

WE all know what we mean by 'lace'. It is a decorative, openwork fabric; and, indeed, this was all it meant to me 15 years ago. Terms like 'Honiton', 'guipure', 'needlepoint' and 'Chantilly' were as meaningless to me as to most people, yet only a century ago they were part of our common general knowledge.

Why was there a change? Fashion is partly to blame, and it is fashion that is responsible for the latest revival of interest. Also responsible for this revival is our greater appreciation of antiques, not only for the craftsmanship that went into them but for their individual character.

It was antiques and an interest in crafts that brought me to lace; one of those happy chances in life when an advertisement in the local paper led me to buy the Brussels needlepoint illustrated in plate 43. From that moment I was captivated and started to look for the information I needed to identify my find.

Anyone who has tried to identify lace from the conflicting information in older books on the subject will appreciate the difficulty I faced. Those coming to the subject now are more fortunate for the recent awakening of interest has led to a number of new books being published, some written by leading authorities.

Why, then, is there a need for another? Because lace has been made throughout Europe for over 400 years in an almost infinite variety of designs and techniques and no one book can do justice to them all.

What I hope to do here is to give a different insight into the more important laces in our history; to show how they differ technically and how their designs have evolved over the centuries. I do not pretend to give all the answers as there is no room here for many of the less fashionable or prestigious laces made for home markets throughout Europe which turn up only occasionally in English collections. Yet once the major types and techniques have been appreciated, it is these oddities which can give an added impetus to collecting.

EXPLANATORY NOTE

LACES, like silver, porcelain and other antiques can be classified by type, their town or country of origin can often be identified and they can be dated with a greater or lesser degree of accuracy. Sadly these tasks are not easy as laces bear no manufacturer's mark and rarely any date. It is only the technical features and style of the lace itself which can provide an answer and, as in other branches of the decorative arts, conscious imitations of earlier styles were made as fashion brought them back into demand.

In this book I have treated each lace type in a separate chapter, listing the technical features which characterize it. Laces which are similar or which might be confused are kept together where possible, but failing this a direction is given as to where they may be found. In particular, the needlepoint laces are all grouped in the initial chapters, the bobbin laces at the end and alternative techniques, such as crochet and embroidered nets, in the centre.

This format means that changes in design cannot be treated in a coherent manner since periods in which different laces were made overlapped. As far as possible, however, within the needlepoint and bobbin sections the laces are discussed in the order in which they developed historically and the illustrations for each major lace type are given in chronological order.

HOW TO IDENTIFY A LACE

Determining the basic technique

LACE is a decorative openwork fabric; but are all decorative openwork fabrics lace? The purist would say not. A true lace is one in which the pattern, and any ground which links the pattern parts, are built up gradually by the interworking of free threads. This excludes textiles such as embroidered nets in which decoration is added to a pre-made fabric.

To make true laces, a variety of techniques are used, each of which creates stitches which are peculiar to that technique and can be discerned in the finished work. The major techniques are those of needlepoint laces and bobbin laces which are explained in general terms on pages 12 and 13 and 14 and 15 respectively. Minor techniques, such as tatting and knitting, are dealt with more briefly in the central chapters of the book. These also include details of other openwork fabrics which may not be true laces but are easily confused with them.

Machine laces are not within the scope of this book but a few examples are shown on pages 182–4, together with the hand-made laces which they imitate. Some distinguishing features are given but, since the range of machine laces is in itself vast, it is easier to pick out the hand-made laces by their own characteristics and to leave a study of machine laces for another occasion.

The initial step, then, when attempting to identify a lace, is to study the stitches and decide, with the aid of the introductory chapters, whether it is a needlepoint or a bobbin lace, or perhaps a mixture of both. If it is none of these, then the central chapters on alternative techniques may give an answer. But beware: machines also create fabrics with some of the characteristics of bobbin laces. So before concluding that you have a hand-made bobbin lace, look at the machine laces on pages 180 and 181 and check that it is not one of these.

Classifying the type or region of origin

The basic techniques of bobbin and needlepoint laces were used in centres scattered throughout Europe and occasionally on other continents. The workers in each region tended to specialize in one technique: thus Venice became famed for her needlepoints, Devon for bobbin laces. Brussels was an exception; here both techniques developed side by side.

In the early years of lace-making, the simple laces from various countries were barely distinguishable from each other but gradually differences in technical detail or design crept in. These were associated with particular towns or regions of origin and gave rise to names by which lace types are still recognized.

The features which distinguish laces fall largely into three categories: the way the pattern is worked; the way the pattern is outlined; and the nature of the ground which connects the pattern parts.

The nature of the ground is particularly useful. The guipure laces (lace in which the pattern areas are connected by bars rather than a mesh, or net, ground) are to be found in the early chapters of the needlepoint section and in the early and later chapters of the bobbin section. The more common net grounds and the laces in which they occur are collated on pages 180–2.

Once a search has been narrowed to a few lace types with similar grounds, consideration must then be given to other features before a final classification can be determined. If the answer is still not clear, the reader must not be disappointed; even the most expert among us cannot always give a categorical answer.

Dating

By identifying a lace type, the date limits for most laces will already have narrowed, but when finer dating is required what matters is the design and the style of an article.

It may be necessary to make a search through the whole of this book or other reference works for a closely-similar design or style of article. Rarely will an exact match be found, but illustrations with features of a similar character to those of the lace under investigation may indicate a range of say 20 to 40 years. Before a conclusion is reached, however, one must bear in mind that many 17th- and 18th-century designs were revived in the 19th century or continued in peasant communities long after they had been discarded by fashionable society.

In very general terms, pointed edgings and geometric designs predominated in the late 16th and early 17th centuries but, as the new century progressed, stylized floral designs appeared and the points broadened into rounded scallops. By the 1650s, straight-edged flounces were being made in the Italian Baroque style, with sweeping curves and scrolls of exotic flowers, but by 1700 designs had degenerated into narrow, trailing lines and curling tendrils.

French influence appeared in the late 17th century with scatterings of small motifs arranged about axes of symmetry but, at the beginning of the 18th century, a new baroque form arose with densely packed, richly patterned designs and strong movement. By the mid 18th century, these designs had opened out into the light-hearted rococo style, which in turn decayed by the end of the century, into tiny flowerheads ranged along the edges of wide expanses of net powdered with dots and sprigs; alternatively it gave way to neo-classical designs.

In the early 19th century the flowerhead motifs grew into curving flower sprays and, in the 1840s, the rococo designs reappeared, soon to be followed by more opulent styles, with massed bunches of naturalistically drawn flowers or heavy guipure laces.

Laces in all these styles, mixed or copied directly, reappeared in the late 19th and early 20th centuries.

A note on threads

Linen thread was used from the 16th century onwards but was largely superseded by cotton in the 19th century, save in better quality laces, as cotton was cheaper and easier to use. In this book I have used the word 'fine' to describe the gauge of the thread as well as its quality.

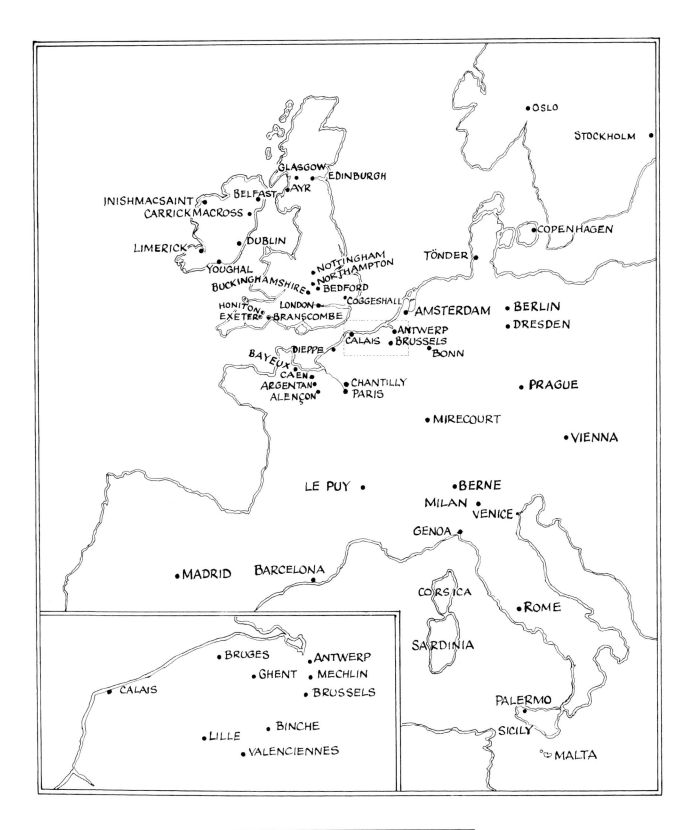

MAP SHOWING THE MAJOR
LACEMAKING CENTRES
OF EUROPE

GLOSSARY

THE meanings of many technical terms have changed over the centuries and, even now, mean different things to different people. This glossary therefore gives the meanings which I attribute to technical terms appearing in this book in order to avoid confusion.

Further technical terms are explained in the introductory chapters on bobbin and needle laces, in the chapters on alternative lace-making techniques, or where they first occur in the text. This is particularly true of items of dress. All such explanations may be found through the index.

Applied/appliqué work   Work in which motifs are attached, usually by sewing, to a base fabric such as a net, to form a design.

Bar or Bride   A cord worked with a needle or bobbins to connect adjacent edges of pattern motifs together.

Buttonhole stitch   This is the basic stitch in needle-point laces and comprises a single thread formed into a loop and twisted once on itself.

Buttonholed bar/bride   A bar or bride covered with buttonhole stitches, usually worked so close together that they touch.

Cloth stitch   A stitch used in bobbin lace to form areas resembling woven material, or cloth. Also called *whole* stitch.

Clothwork   An area resembling woven material. This term should strictly be reserved for bobbin laces where the clothwork is made by cloth stitch, but it is also used for densely worked pattern areas in needlepoints.

Cordonnet   The raised outline on the right side of a needle lace. Also applied to the raised outline of some bobbin laces.

Couching   A technique in which a thread, or group of threads, is sewn on to a surface by a different thread.

Drawn-thread work   An embroidery technique on a woven fabric in which the embroidery threads are used to draw the fabric threads apart and so create decorative openwork patterns of holes and stitching. Also known as pulled work but in this book I have used the term 'pulled work' for a different technique.

Filling (Filling stitch)   A fancy stitch usually employed to fill a small area within a pattern to create a decorative effect. There is an enormous variety of such stitches. Also known by the French terms *mode* and *à jours*.

Footing   A narrow tape provided along that edge of a lace which is to be attached to a garment or other article to take the strain of the sewing. It is sometimes worked integrally with the lace but is often sewn on so that it can be replaced when damaged.

Footside   That edge of a lace intended to be attached to a garment or other article.

Gimp   A bobbin-lace thread which is thicker than the majority of threads in a lace. This is an East Midlands term but is used throughout this book for similar threads.

Ground   The linking part of a lace which connects the pattern motifs. It consists of a series of bars in a guipure lace, a network of fine meshes, or a machine-made net.

Guipure   Any lace in which the pattern motifs are close together and linked either where they touch or by bars connecting adjacent edges and in which relatively large openings are left. Tape and geometric laces where connecting bars form part of the pattern are included.

Half stitch   A bobbin-lace stitch used *inter alia* to create areas of grille-like structure. See plate 4.

Headside   The free edge of a lace opposite the footside.

Insertion   A strip of lace with a footside along both edges sewn between two lengths of fabric to form a decorative seam.

à Jours   *See* Filling.

Leadwork   A decorative bobbin-lace stitch in which one thread is woven back and forth between three others, usually forming a square-ended spot or rectangle. This is the usual Honiton name for a stitch more commonly called a *tally* or *point d'esprit* in East Midlands laces. Other names include *leaf* and *wheatear* but I prefer to use these for spots with pointed ends.

Mode   *See* Filling.

Needleweaving   An embroidery technique in which a thread is darned back and forth through two or more other threads to create a woven structure. A similar effect can be created in bobbin laces.

Overcasting   An embroidery technique in which a sewing thread is taken over and under a thread, or group of threads, repeatedly in a helix to strengthen the thread or bind threads together. Also known as *whipping* or *oversewing*.

Picot   A decorative point or loop often used to decorate raised work, edges or bars. Also called *purl* or *pearl*.
Picoted bar/bride   A bar, or bride, decorated with picots.
Point d'esprit   *See* Leadwork.
Point de racroc   A general name for a bobbin stitch used to join two panels of bobbin lace together invisibly. The stitch varies according to the type of lace being joined.

Pulled-thread work   An embroidery technique on a woven fabric in which some threads are pulled out of the fabric to leave open areas crossed by other threads which are drawn together, strengthened and decorated by embroidery threads. Also known as drawn-thread work but in this book I have used the term drawn-thread work for an alternative technique.

Raised work   Three-dimensional detail on the right side of a lace.

Sewing   A stitch used to join a pair of bobbin-lace threads to an edge. One thread of the pair is pulled through the edge with a pin or hook to form a loop then the bobbin carrying the other thread is passed through the loop to link the two threads to the edge.

Tally   *See* Leadwork.

Wheatear   *See* Leadwork.
Whole stitch   *See* Cloth stitch.

IT may be difficult to appreciate that an entire fabric can be built up with a single needle and thread, but this is how needlepoint lace is made. It is created on a design which would formerly have been drawn on parchment but is now more usually drawn on card or oiled cloth. This was often called a pricking because stiff parchments were pricked with holes around outlines of the design, but, to avoid confusion with bobbin-lace prickings, I shall follow current usage and call it the pattern.

To start the lace, the pattern is tacked on to two layers of fabric and foundation threads are laid over the

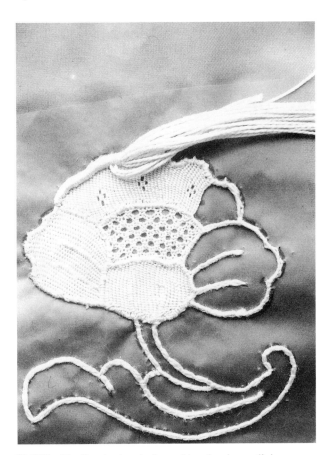

PLATE 1: Needlepoint lace in the making showing outlining threads couched down on to a pattern with areas of the design filled in with different stitches. Part of the outline is being raised by the addition of surface threads covered with closely spaced buttonhole stitching.

surface, along the lines of the design. These foundation threads are couched down with additional threads passing over the foundation threads and through the pattern and underlying fabric to hold them in place. Eventually, when the work has been completed, the foundation threads remain within the lace while the couching threads are cut between the two layers of fabric to release the lace from the pattern, and are then removed.

Once the foundation threads have been secured, the spaces within and around the design motifs are filled with needlework, mainly in variations on the buttonhole stitch. Often the ground, or background part of a lace holding the motifs together is worked first, and then the motifs are completed.

In guipure laces, the motifs are closely spaced and joined both where they touch and by short bars which cross the spaces between them. In their simplest form, these bars comprise a thread sewn to the outline of one motif, taken across the space to a neighbouring motif and returned to the first motif. More usually, this simple bar is strengthened by buttonhole stitches worked tightly together along it and projecting points or loops, called picots, are often added as decoration. Where space permits, several bars may meet or cross to form coarse meshes.

In other laces, the ground consists of a network of fine meshes created by loosely worked buttonhole stitches. These are formed in rows linked into the foundation threads which outline the motifs and are arranged to fill the spaces between them. Although most needlepoint laces have a needle-made ground, in some Brussels laces the needlepoint motifs are connected by a bobbin-made ground or are applied to a machine-made net.

The design itself is filled in with areas of close stitching and with more open work to enliven it. The close stitching is worked over threads stretched across the pattern and linked to the foundation threads. When tightly worked, the stretched threads are completely hidden and the resulting structure resembles woven fabric: this is known as 'clothwork'. In looser work, the loops of the buttonhole stitches and underlying stretched threads can still be seen, at least with a magnifying glass.

A more open work is created by different groupings of buttonhole stitches, some worked on stretched threads, others looped into previous stitches or formed into rings or stars. All these fancy variations are known as filling stitches, *modes*, or *à jours*.

Once the ground and the design have been completed, the lace may be released immediately from the pattern. The result is a flat lace, an essentially two-dimensional structure. Alternatively, before being released from the pattern, the lace may be embellished with raised work. This involves further threads being attached to the surface of the lace, usually around its outlines.

The surface threads may in themselves constitute the raised work but often they are covered with, or attached by, buttonhole stitches and frills of picots are added. A clear result of this process is that the top, or right, side of a raised needlepoint lace is very different from the reverse, or wrong side.

Some appreciation may now have been gained of the work that goes into a needlepoint lace, but the story is not yet finished. The completed lace with its design, ground and raised work, now released from its pattern, is often only a small part of a collar or flounce and must be joined to other parts of a design to make a finished, usable article. For this purpose, all the fragments of a design must be assembled, tacked on to a master pattern and sewn together invisibly.

In amateur work today, all these stages in a needlepoint lace will be completed by the same person but this was not always so. Lace could be made more quickly, more expertly and with greater uniformity by a group of workers each of whom specialized in a particular stitch or task. This was particularly true of the French industry where as many as 20 workers were employed on any one article, from the initial drawing of the design to the lifting of the lace from the pattern, the removal of the couching threads and the packing for sale.

PLATE 2: **Detail of a needlepoint guipure showing the pattern motifs connected by brides covered with closely spaced buttonhole stitches. The raised outline is covered with similar stitching.**

GENERAL CHARACTERISTICS OF BOBBIN LACES

WHILE needlepoint laces are made with a single needle and thread, bobbin laces are made with a multitude of threads each carried on a small rod, or bobbin. The bobbins, which are 8–16 cm (3–6 in) long and usually made of bone or wood, have a neck at one end on which the thread is wound and are manipulated by their other ends to weave, cross and plait the threads together. The bobbins are in fact worked in pairs, one thread being carried between two bobbins. This simplifies the starting of a lace as the pair of bobbins

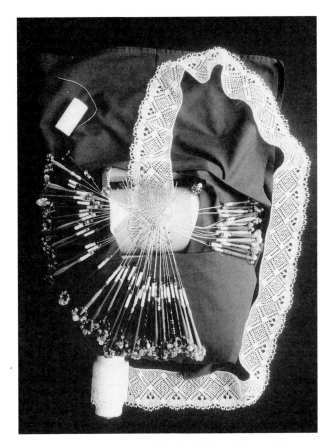

PLATE 3: Straight torchon bobbin lace being made on a pricking fixed around a French roller pillow.

The roller is seated in the pillow so that it can rotate and allows the pattern to be worked continuously: on a flat, English pillow, once the length of a pricking has been completed, the lace must be removed and repinned at the top of the pricking before the next length can be worked. The bobbins, with their rings of glass beads, called spangles, are English East Midlands bobbins.

can be hung from a pin fixed into a pattern to be worked and avoids the need for knots or loose ends.

In bobbin-lace making, the pattern is always called a pricking since its pinholes are essential for locating the pins which keep the threads in place as work progresses. The pins are pushed through the pricking into a hard, straw-stuffed pillow which gives the lace its other name of 'pillow lace'. This, however, is somewhat misleading as needlepoints may also be supported on a pillow during working.

Bobbin laces, like needlepoints, comprise a design of motifs interconnected by a ground of bars or net which holds the lace together. The motifs are usually worked in a stitch called whole, or cloth, stitch since it forms a structure like a woven cloth although half stitch, which gives a grille-like effect, is sometimes used (see Plate 4). Areas of fancy, or filling, stitches often enliven the design as they do in needlepoint laces.

Although all bobbin laces contain the same basic stitches, they can be subdivided into three main groups: 'part laces', 'straight laces' and a third group which combines features of the other two and which is sometimes called 'semi-straight'.

Straight bobbin laces

A straight lace is one in which the entirety of the pattern and the ground of net or brides which joins the pattern motifs together is made in one continuous process. The result is usually a straight length of lace in which the design is repeated, although curved and corner pieces can also be made. The pattern is often outlined with a thick, or gimp, thread which is incorporated during the working of the lace itself.

Such 'straight' laces are distinguished from part and semi-straight laces in that threads continue from the ground into the pattern areas and out into the ground again. Also, in the clothwork pattern areas, the threads lie roughly at right angles to each other and parallel and perpendicular to the length of the lace whereas, in part and semi-straight laces, the threads follow the twists and turns in the design ignoring the general direction or extent of the pattern. Furthermore, the two sides of a straight lace are usually almost indistinguishable although, occasionally, tallies (see Plate 163) are worked over the surface on the right side. This type of 'raised' work is very different from the raised outlines common in part laces (see Plate 91) and in needle-points.

Although only a few bobbins (usually between 20 and 40) are needed for simple straight laces, several hundred may be used for complex patterns. The maximum workable width of a straight lace is limited to about 20 cm (8 in) and large items must be made in strips or sections which are subsequently joined together.

Part bobbin laces

In part-lace making, individual motifs, such as flower sprigs or small areas of a design, are worked on separate prickings. When all the parts have been completed, they are arranged upside down on a master pattern to be joined together. To facilitate this joining, the motifs are often made with an openwork surround to which the ground threads can be linked.

As in needlepoint laces, the ground may consist of bars, to form a guipure, or a network of meshes. It may be made with bobbins but in the 19th century it was quite commonly needle-made. Alternatively, the motifs may be sewn to a net made by hand or machine.

With this technique, there is no limit to the overall size of the finished piece of lace and any number of workers may be employed in making individual motifs. The motifs themselves require comparatively few bobbins (between 20 and 60).

The part technique also allows raised edges to be created on the right side of the work; these may comprise simple bundles of threads or strips of bobbin-made clothwork (see Plates 91 and 107) and distinguish part laces from straight laces. A gimp thread is sometimes incorporated as in straight laces.

Semi-straight bobbin laces

Semi-straight laces, like straight laces, are made in continuous lengths but the threads follow the pattern round twists and turns in the design and, where parts touch or lie close together, threads currently being worked are looped into the previously made edge to join them together. This technique is also used in part laces and is called 'taking a sewing' (see Glossary under Sewing). It is also used to link in additional threads to form decorative fillings or a net or bar ground.

Semi-straight laces are often made in meandering tape designs but are distinguished from laces made with machine tapes by the way the threads are worked smoothly round corners, with no puckering or folding of the material, by changes in the width of the tape and the incorporation of different filling stitches within it.

Changes in width are sometimes accomplished by the addition or removal of threads during working; this is a common practice in part lace making but rarer in straight laces.

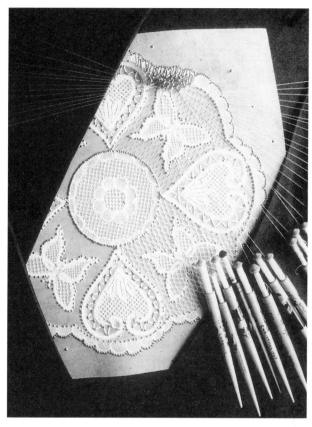

PLATE 4: Completed motifs of an East Devon (Honiton) part lace are pinned on a pricking and are being joined together by a net ground.

The outlines of the hearts and butterflies are worked in whole, or cloth stitch, while the more open frame is worked in half, or grille stitch.

Note the variety of fancy filling stitches within the motifs, including leadworks (tallies) in zigzag lines in the hearts.

By kind permission of Lorraine Coram

I
NEEDLEPOINT LACES

RETICELLA EMBROIDERIES

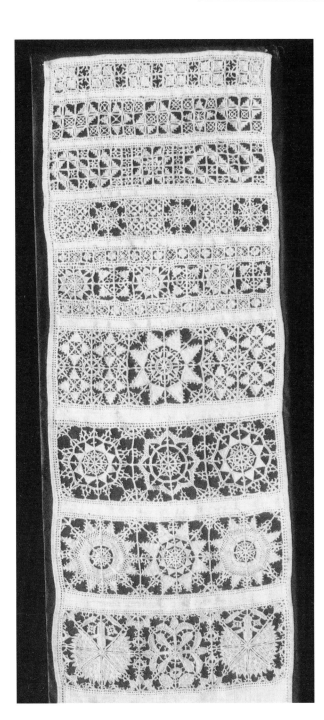

PLATE 5: Sampler of reticella needlework: English: 1650–1700.
   Width 15–16 cm (6 in)
   Length 47.5 cm (18.7 in)
The woven linen fabric can be seen around the edges of the sampler and in the horizontal bands between the strips of reticella embroidery. All the reticella patterns include distinct horizontal and vertical lines where the foundation threads of the linen fabric are strengthened with needleweaving; but the rosettes also have distinct diagonal lines due to needleweaving on added foundation threads thrown across the open squares.

Collection of Mrs Kathleen Tipping

Characteristics

1. Openwork embroidery in rectangular areas surrounded by bands of woven fabric with threads extending from the fabric into the embroidery.
2. Grids of needlewoven lines cross the patterns at right-angles to the edges.
3. Repeated patterns of geometric designs, stylized flowers or other motifs with angular outlines created by button-holed, needlewoven and overcast bars with small areas filled with buttonhole stitches.
4. Cut edges of woven fabric neatened by overcasting.

Points to watch

Reticella cutwork embroidery, braid-based reticella (pages 20–1) and the early style of free needlepoint lace called punto in aria (pages 22–4), were made in very similar designs and only the technical basis of the work distinguishes them. Look for the woven fabric with threads continuing into the design for reticella, the plaited braids of braid-based reticella and absence of these features in punto in aria.

A variation on reticella embroidery used a knotted buttonhole stitch in very densely-worked areas and was sometimes known as 'punto groppo' or 'punto avorio'.

History

Openwork fabrics were made in Egyptian and other early civilizations but the story of lace as we know it begins in Europe in the 16th century. This, for the aristocracy, was a period of particular ostentation in dress, when rich fabrics, used in profusion, were further enriched with embroidery and couched braids of gold, silver and silk threads.

Linen undergarments, too, were decorated where they showed at the neck and wrists, often with blackwork embroidery, sometimes with insertions of knotted or filet lace (pages 68–9). Gradually, forms of whitework embroidery developed in which holes were pierced in the linen, threads withdrawn or small areas cut away to form various openwork fabrics.

By the second half of the century, large areas of fabric were being cut away and the spaces filled with needlework. Since the embroidery was based on the remaining threads of the linen which divided the areas into squares and rectangles

PLATE 6: Detail of Plate 7b showing: horizontal bands of woven linen with cut edges neatened by overcasting; horizontal and vertical needlewoven bars worked on threads of the woven linen remaining in the pattern; overcast and buttonhole-stitched bars and picots.

and formed a foundation for the work, the natural tendency was to form repeated geometric designs. These continued, growing in elaboration, until well into the 17th century.

Much of this work was carried out by amateurs for whom pattern books, such as *Les Singuliers et Nouveaux Pourtraicts et Ouvrages de Lingerie* by Frederic de Vinciolo, Paris 1587, were available. There were also considerable bodies of professional workers, particularly in Flanders and in Italy where this extreme form of cutwork came to be known as 'reticella', meaning a small grid or network.

It was these cutwork and reticella embroideries that came to decorate the wide ruffs, standing collars and associated cuffs fashionable particularly in Spain and northern Europe in the late 16th and early 17th centuries. Here the geometric patterns persisted even though more flowing designs, often with trailing plant forms, had started to creep into Italian work before the turn of the century. Such designs also incorporated animals, birds and people, which were often rather naïvely drawn and arranged at odd angles, with little concern for the relative scale of features portrayed.

FIGURE 1: Late 16th-century woman's ruff and cap.
Ruffs were made up from pleated lengths of fine lawn often adorned with reticella embroidery and finished with a pointed edging of punto in aria (Plate 8), or of bobbin lace (Plate 73). They were worn equally by men and women and grew in size until, by the early 17th century, they were so enormous that they have been likened to cartwheels.

In the 16th century smaller versions of the ruff were often worn at the wrist but by the 17th century these were largely superseded by the turned-back cuffs, still decorated with embroidery and lace.

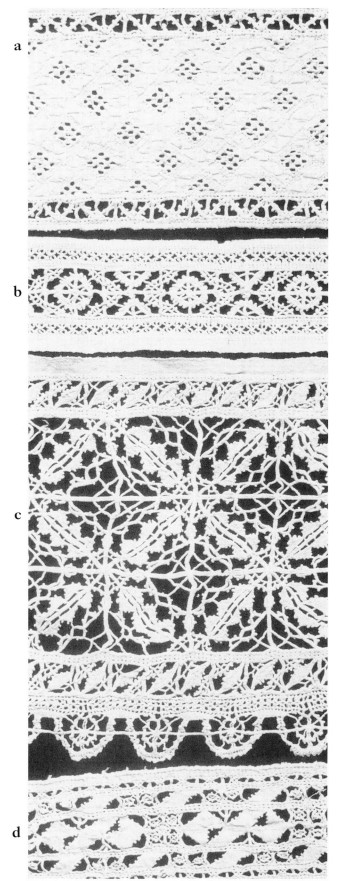

a

b

c

d

PLATE 7:

a.   Linen band with pierced and embroidered whitework decoration and cutwork embroidery along the long edges: late 16th C–early 17th C.
   Depth 11.5 cm (4.5 in)
This is a coarse example for furnishing use.

b.   Linen band with reticella embroidery: late 16th century.
   Overall depth 5.5 cm (2.2 in)
This piece is of fine quality and could have been made for dress or for household use. (See Plate 6 for detail.)

c.   Linen flounce with reticella embroidery and scalloped lower edging of bobbin lace: 17th C.
   Depth of reticella 17 cm (7 in)
   Depth of lower bobbin lace edging 3 cm (1.2 in)
This is a coarse work of a type made and used as a furnishing lace, particularly for church linen, throughout the 17th century.

d.   Linen band with reticella embroidery: about 1600.
   Depth 6 cm (2.5 in)
The very closely worked triangles in this piece are particularly associated with Italian work.

PLATE 8 (RIGHT):

a.   (*top*; see Plate 11 for detail). Linen band with reticella embroidery and a pointed edging of punto in aria (pp. 22–23): about 1600.
   Depth of linen with reticella work 5.5 cm (2.2 in)
   Depth of punto in aria 2.5 cm (1 in)
Note the figures in the reticella and punto in aria.

b.   (*bottom left*). Linen or cotton band with reticella embroidery and a pointed edging of punto in aria: late 19th C–20th C.
   Depth of reticella 5 cm (2 in)
   Depth of punto in aria 4.5 cm (1.7 in)
There is little to distinguish this piece from the 17th-century work which it copies. One clue is the coarseness and openesss of the work which might suggest it is a 17th-century furnishing lace but then one would expect a less acutely pointed edging.

c.   (*bottom right*). Square of reticella embroidery; 20th C.
   Width 8 cm (3.2 in)
The frayed edges show that this has been cut out of a piece of fabric. The large scale of the design as well as the feel of the thread indicate that it is a late copy.

As well as making a suitable costume lace, reticella was widely used to decorate household linen, where it was often combined with bands of drawn or pulled thread work, other forms of cutwork embroidery and with filet lace. In Catholic Europe, considerable quantities were made for church use, and, in this conservative field, the geometric designs persisted long after fashion had turned to the flowing, exotic world of the baroque. The persistence in domestic work is shown particularly in English whitework samplers (Plate 5), many of which still exist and appear to date from the second half of the 17th century.

By the early 18th century, reticella was entirely outmoded in northern Europe, but it continued to be made in peasant communities, particularly in the Greek Islands. The large scale of the designs and the clumsier workmanship often distinguish these laces from their fashionable predecessors but many are datable only to within the 18th or 19th centuries.

The dating of reticella is particularly difficult today; the elaboration of design and quality of workmanship in the early laces depended not only on their date but also on their country of manufacture, their intended use and the personal taste and wealth of their owners. Added to this is a further complication. The lively interest in antiques in the late 19th century and the revolt of the Arts and Crafts movement against machine-made products in general led to a revival of interest in many forms of lace-making, including reticella embroidery.

In many countries this manifested itself in a wealth of amateur work, often in cotton thread on machine-woven cotton which is readily distinguishable from the early linen lace. Much finer work was also done in various centres in Europe, sometimes in linen thread, in designs taken directly from the old pattern books. In Great Britain an industry was based in the Lake District where cloth was again being woven on hand looms from hand-spun linen thread. The product was renamed 'Ruskin Work' after one of the leading member of the Arts and Crafts movement.

Many of these later reticellas are now over a century old and not easily distinguishable from their earlier counterparts. Even the expert, with long experience, cannot always be sure.

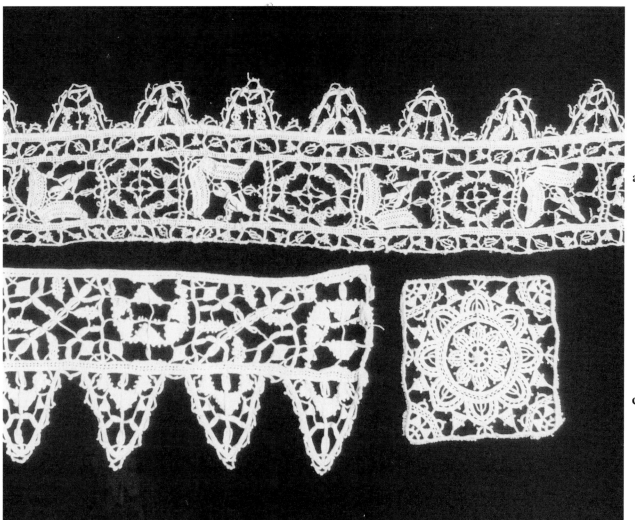

a

b

c

BRAID-BASED RETICELLA EMBROIDERY

Characteristics

1. Foundation grid of plaited braids at right angles to each other and possibly also along shaped edges.

2. Repeated patterns of geometric designs, stylized flowers or other motifs with angular outlines created by buttonholed, needlewoven and overcast bars with small areas filled with buttonhole stitches.

3. Free edges are often dentate (finished with a row of points), or scalloped, with a symmetrical motif filling each point or scallop.

Points to watch

See under reticella cutwork embroidery (page 17).

History

At some time during the development of reticella embroideries it must have become apparent that a great deal of time, and hence money, was being wasted in spinning thread and weaving fabric which was to be cut out and thrown away. Why not forget the fabric altogether?

One alternative developed was a grid of plaited braids couched on to a pattern to provide the foundation for the embroidery which, in all other respects, was identical to true reticella embroidery. This form of work did not oust the true reticella but was made alongside it, to the same designs and for the same uses and, like true reticella, was made in Italy, Flanders, England and other parts of Europe.

FIGURE 2: Early 17th-century woman's standing collar.
In the late 16th and early 17th centuries an alternative fashion to the ruff was a standing collar which was starched and supported by a wire underframe. Like the ruff it was often decorated with reticella embroidery and a punto in aria or bobbin lace edging. The man's version was closed around the neck but a woman's often left the throat bare and a matching edging was worn around the low-cut neckline of the bodice.

PLATE 9:
a.   Edging of braid-based reticella: about 1640–50.
   Depth of scallop 6 cm (2.4 in)
The plaited foundation braids can be seen along the top edge and
around the motifs in the scallops. The tightness of working of the
buttonhole stitches in the design suggests that this is an Italian
piece.

b.   Edging of braid-based reticella: about 1640–60.
   Depth of scallop 10 cm (4 in)
The looseness of working of the buttonhole stitches and manner in
which the design fills the space available suggest a Northern origin
for this piece: the rather naïve, sketchy drawing suggests it is
English.
   The shallow scallop in both 9a and 9b dates them to the mid-
17th century.

PUNTO IN ARIA AND
EARLY FLEMISH NEEDLEPOINT

PLATE 10: Flounce of punto in aria: 1620–4
Width 16.5 cm (6.5 in)
Length shown 38 cm (15 in)

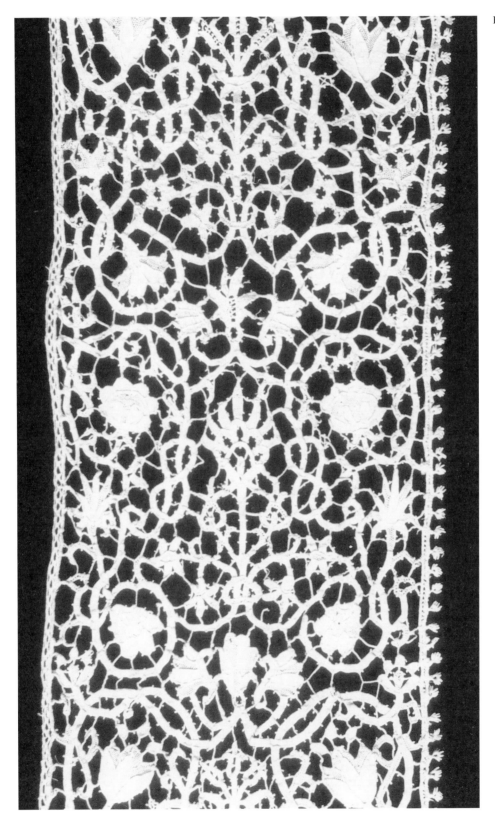

Characteristics (punto in aria)
1. Guipure needlepoint lace mainly in buttonhole stitch.
2. Designs:
   a. Geometric, like reticella (pages 16–21).
   b. Stylized flowerheads and other motifs connected by trailing stems and buttonholed brides.
3. Often found as pointed or scalloped edgings with a symmetrical design repeated in each point or scallop.
4. Lines in slight relief are fairly common – these are formed by needlewoven foundation threads within the design or closely buttonholed threads on the surface, around or within the design.

Points to watch (punto in aria)
See under reticella cutwork embroidery (page 17). Punto in aria is often found as an edging to reticella embroidery.

Punto in aria is strictly speaking an Italian needlepoint but similar laces were made throughout Europe. Italian work can sometimes be distinguished by the density and stiffness of its clothwork areas due to the extreme tightness of working of the buttonhole stitches. The looser, more supple Flemish and English work can be seen in Plates 13 and 9 respectively.

The type of trailing-stem design shown in Plate 10 was also carried out in the contemporary 'mezzo punto' technique (see tape laces – pages 60–1 and Plate 12). The closely-woven tapes were embellished with needle-worked bars, fillings and raised outlines and the result is easily mistaken for punto in aria.

History (punto in aria)
Punto in aria, meaning 'stitch in the air', is the Italian name for the first true needlepoint lace which was made without a woven or plaited foundation. It began in the form of separate, decorative points around the neck and sleeve openings of the linen shirt, or chemise, worn by both men and women in the 16th century. An example of this work is seen in Plate 8a and in the detail in Plate 11 which shows how the free needlepoint is linked into the edge of the linen band but is otherwise unsupported by it.

Gradually the points grew larger and more elaborate, as did the areas of cutwork and reticella embroideries which they frequently edged, and it is this combination of work which is often seen in the portraiture of the late 16th and early 17th centuries. By 1600 the early, sharply triangular outline of the points had generally softened and broadened into the shape of a gothic arch, but this is not a fixed rule for identification. Vinciolo's Pattern Book of 1587 shows many designs for arched and scalloped edgings whereas a man's standing collar in the Rijksmuseum, Amsterdam has a pointed edging and is dated to about 1610. The constant feature throughout this period is the use of repeated or alternating designs within the points or scallops, always with a line of symmetry through the point, whether the design be geometric or floral.

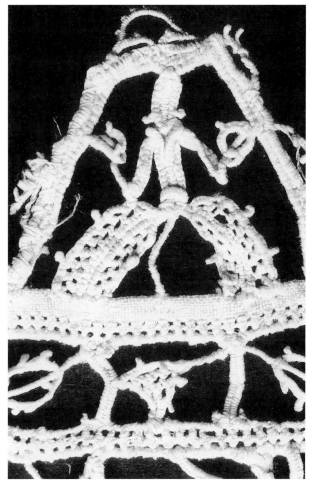

PLATE 11: **Detail of the punto in aria edging in Plate 8a.**
   Depth of point 2.5 cm (1 in)
The foundation threads of the lacework are sewn directly into the edge of the linen fabric. The man depicted in the design wears the typical full breeches of the period. The collar and belt details are worked in loose threads over the surface.

As technical expertise increased in what was still a relatively new craft, the lace makers progressed from making separate points to continuous lengths of lace. These were used in the same way as reticella and, though lacking the constraints of a fabric foundation, were made in the same compartmented designs. Only gradually did stems of floral designs trail from one compartment to the next.

By the 1620s, designs of simple flowerheads borne on flowing, curving stems were common but the element of symmetry still remained. In Italy, the buttonholed clothwork was tightly worked, the stems narrow, of even width and often bounded by a raised outline leaving clearly defined spaces between the pattern motifs. The floral designs did, however, provide some broader pattern areas which could be enlivened with fancy filling stitches. These were few at first but presage the delights of the second half of the century.

PLATE 12: **Point of gothic-arch shape from an edging of mezzo punto: Italian, 1620–40.**
  Depth of point 12.5 cm (5 in)
It was only when I came to examine this piece thoroughly during research on this book that I realized that it is a tape lace, made with a combination of closely woven tapes and very tightly worked buttonhole stitches. The design is typical of Italian punto in aria of the period.

Early Flemish Needlepoint

The development of free needlepoint laces was not confined to Italy. Flanders was also a centre for the industry and designs followed much the same trends as in Italy in the early part of the 17th century.

It is not always possible, even for the expert, to distinguish work from the two areas; but, in general: Flemish clothwork tends to be more loosely worked than the Italian; Flemish designs are not outlined with tightly-worked buttonhole stitches; the Flemish floral motifs tend to be more expansive and fill a greater proportion of the lace than Italian motifs; the overall feel of the Flemish work is one of suppleness compared with the firmness and crispness of Italian work.

In the mid- to late 17th century, Flanders does not appear to have followed Venice's lead in the making of raised needlepoints (pages 28–9). Instead, flat points continued to be made but in the designs of the Flemish bobbin laces popular in the Low Countries (page 132).

FIGURE 3: **Man's falling collar (or band); about 1625–50.**
In the early 17th century the stiff ruffs and standing collars were gradually replaced by the softer line of the falling band. The man's collar fastened high around the neck and often had a linen centre. From this a broad scalloped border of lace fell in a smooth curve on to the back and shoulders. At the front it was often gathered around two corners and met at a front opening but shaped designs for the corners were also available and displayed the patterns to best advantage. Women's dress of the period is shown in Figure 12 (page 84).

PLATE 13: Corner fragment of Flemish needlepoint: 1725–50.
   Overall length 42 cm (17 in)
The broader scallop of this piece suggests that it is slightly later in
date than the fragment shown in Plate 12. A Northern origin is
suggested by the looser working of the stitches and absence of
tight outlining which give it a suppleness not found in Italian
work; the general quality of design and workmanship indicate a
professional, Flemish origin. Note the use of light, overcast bars
instead of buttonholed bars and the surface decoration around the
flower centres.

VENETIAN NEEDLEPOINTS

Flat point

a

b

c

d

Characteristics

1. Guipure needlepoint lace.
2. Essentially a flat lace but thicker foundation threads within the work give rise to pronounced lines around and within the pattern areas.
3. Clothwork pattern areas of tightly-worked buttonhole stitches often enlivened with geometric arrangements of holes (*see* Plate 15).
4. Buttonholed brides, often decorated with rings and picots, interconnect the pattern areas.
5. Scrolling 17th-century baroque and branching coralline designs.

Point to watch

Raised work (see pages 28–31) was often added to flat points in the 19th century.

History of Venetian needlepoints

By the mid-17th century Venice was already famed for her needlepoints. Her workers, mostly convent trained, made a good deal of the punto in aria exported to the rest of Europe and we have already seen how its style changed from the geometric to more freely-flowing forms. From these there was a natural progression to the continuous movement of the Italian baroque, a style already well-established in other applied arts.

In Venice this style was interpreted in two ways: in the flat points seen in Plates 14 and 15 and in the more elaborate rose points (rose here meaning raised) seen in Plates 16 to 19. In bolder designs, not illustrated, large-scale exotic flowers and broad, scrolling leaves undulate continuously across the entire surface of the fabric, while backward-curling

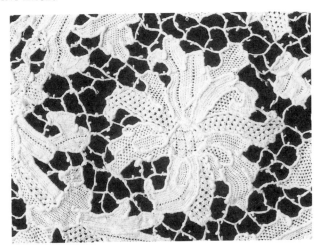

PLATE 15: Detail of Plate 14a.
Note the thick lines due to foundation threads within the work and the use of filling stitches to enliven the design; these are formed by patterns of holes in the clothwork and thus differ from the filling stitches worked in spaces between the motifs in many 18th- and 19th-century needlepoints.

branches bring the motifs into close proximity and reduce the need for connecting brides. Heavy raised work incorporated in these designs gives the form sometimes known as 'gros point'.

In lighter forms the motifs are smaller, the connecting brides more numerous and often interlinked and decorated with picoted rings. The dense clothwork is enlivened with more varied filling stitches while frills of picots around the padded outlines add richness to the effect.

It has generally been assumed that the bolder gros point appeared first and decayed gradually through the lighter rose point into attenuated designs of curling tendrils and coral-like branches which were current at the end of the century. Certainly this is the underlying trend but portraiture of the period shows that the gros point coexisted with the lighter laces for most of the second half of the 17th century and it continued to be made, particularly for church and furnishing uses, into the 18th century.

By the end of the 17th century, fashions had changed; clear designs which displayed well in flat expanses, as in the man's rabat collar of the 1650s to 1670s (see Figure 13), were no longer needed for the cravats and gathered frills of the 1690s. Texture was more important than pattern and this trend reached its extreme in the raised needlepoint known as 'point de neige'. In this, what little form was left to the design was hidden beneath a froth of picoted rings and crescents scattered indiscriminately over the surface.

By 1700 the Venetian industry which only two or three decades earlier had produced the most expensive, prestigious and sought-after laces in Europe was in decline. The Italianate baroque style was outmoded and was to remain so for the next 150 years.

The return came in the 1850s when guipures and heavier

PLATE 14: These four pieces show the general design trend in Venetian laces from the stronger, baroque style of the mid-17th century to the decadent form of about 1700.

Length shown 25 cm (10 in)

a. Flat point edging: 1660–90.
    Depth 10 cm (4 in)
    Pattern repeat 40 cm (15.5 in)
The design flows almost continuously from one repeat to the next.

b. Flat point edging: 1670–90.
    Depth 10 cm (4 in)
    Pattern repeat 46.5 cm (18.5 in)
The curving baroque lines are still visible but the pattern repeats are separated and on a smaller scale than in Plate 14a.

c. Flat point edging: 1680–1700.
    Depth 3 cm (1.5 in)
    Pattern repeat 40 cm (16 in)

d. Fragment of flat point: about 1700.
    Size shown: depth 7.5 cm (3 in)
This lace has been cut and rejoined at a later date but the indeterminate design of tiny dissociated scrolls means that this is not readily apparent.

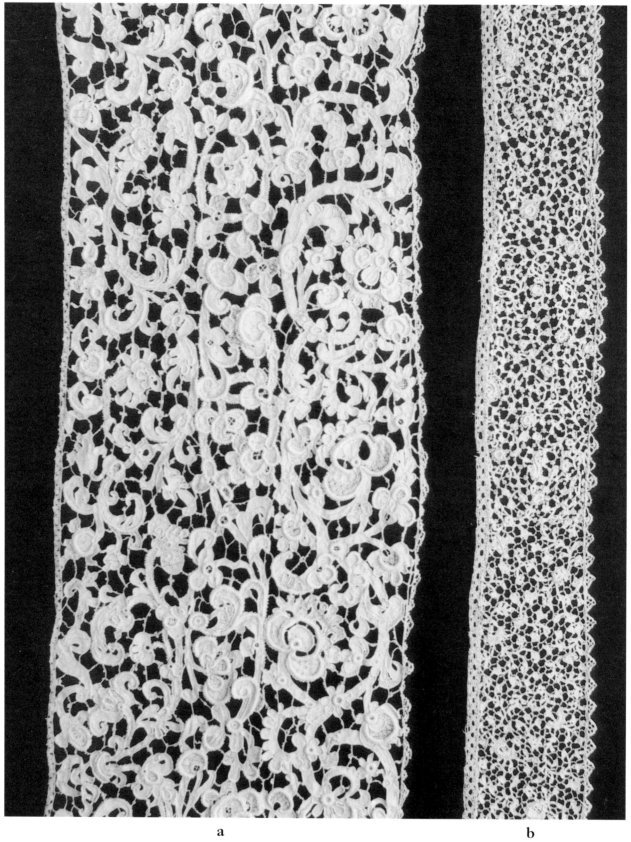

a   b

laces generally came back into fashion. Old needlepoints were rediscovered, unpicked and the techniques relearnt in various centres. Although the modern copies were slow to catch on, by the late 1870s and 1880s these copies, together with antique originals whose motifs were cut and re-ordered to suit the current styles, formed a growing part of the needlepoint market. Innishmacsaint and New Ross in Ireland, Burano in the Venetian lagoon and various Belgian towns were only some of the centres which included 'Venetian' laces in their repertoires.

VENETIAN ROSE (RAISED) POINT

Characteristics

Venetian rose point is essentially Venetian flat point (pages 26–7) with the addition of raised work formed by buttonhole stitches over padding couched on to the surface. The varied nature of the padding gives different effects:

1. A single thread or a few threads buttonholed over often outline the design.
2. A thick but almost uniform core of a multitude of threads forms snakelike convolutions which outline or complement the design underneath. Closely-worked buttonhole stitches form a smooth surface over this but may be decorated with picoted frills (Plate 17).
3. Carefully graduated padding forms crescents which are thick in the centre and narrow towards the ends. The surface is smooth and frills are sometimes added as shown in Plate 18.
4. Tiny padded rings and curves are scattered over the surface and overwhelmed by picoted frills (Plate 19).

PLATE 16 (LEFT):

a. (left). Flounce of Venetian rose point: 1660–90.
   Depth 23 cm (9 in)
   Length shown 51 cm (20 in)
The flounce has been made up from three strips of rose point joined edge to edge, probably in the late 19th century. A number of brides have been remade but the flow of the design within each strip is still visible; in many pieces altered in the 19th century the motifs are completely rearranged so that the original design is lost.

b. (right). Rose point edging: 1690–1710.
   Depth 8 cm (3 in) (including bobbin-made footing)
This edging is made from two strips joined end to end. Both have been cut down from their original depths as shown by the way the pattern is sliced through where the strips are joined to their later footing and heading. Both show the random patterning of the turn of the 17th century; the flurries of raised work and ornamented brides are not quite sufficient for this to be called 'point de neige'. Note the way the brides in the lower edging form irregular meshes.

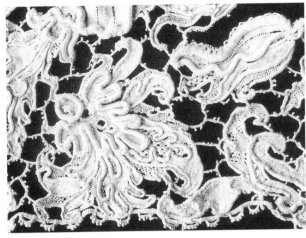

PLATE 17: Detail of the rose point shown on the cover, probably Venetian, with convoluted, padded raised work. The bundle of threads used to form the padding can best be seen in Plate 1 and in the tape-lace detail in Plate 50.

PLATE 18: Detail of the flounce in Plate 16a showing the beautifully formed, padded crescent with frills of picots, typical of Venetian work.

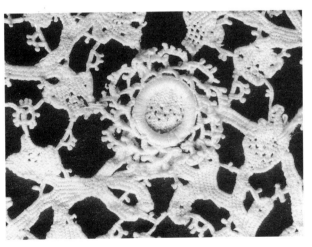

PLATE 19: Detail of the upper edging in Plate 16b.

In many cases these late examples are easily distinguishable from the originals: the thread and workmanship are coarser, the designs are adapted to the shapes of 19th- and 20th-century costume items and are often inspired by, rather than copied from, the originals. But there are also direct copies, made with fine linen thread to a technical standard nearing perfection; only a certain stiffness of style and over-elaboration of detail distinguish these from the originals.

Points to watch

Venetian rose point is essentially a 17th-century lace but close copies were made in needlepoint, crochet and by machine in the 19th and 20th centuries.

The raised work in original Venetian needlepoints is worked into the lace during manufacture. In the 19th century, raised work was often added to earlier flat points but the threads sewing the new work to the old can often be distinguished on the back.

The snakelike form of raised work described in 2 (above) has often been ascribed to Spanish laces. In fact, it was probably a transitional form between the simple raised outline described in 1 and the beautifully modelled crescents described in 3 but it continued in use after the crescents had developed and was used by workers in other parts of Europe who copied the prestigious Venetian laces.

Many French needlepoints (pages 32–4) were made in the Italian baroque manner in the 1660s–1670s until a new French classical style was introduced, after which both centres copied each other's laces to some extent. It is often difficult to distinguish between them.

PLATE 20:

a.   Edging: copy of Venetian rose point with a bobbin-made footing: late 19th C.
   Depth of needlepoint 6.5 cm (2.7 in)
   Pattern repeat 33.5 cm (13.5 in)
   Length shown 32 cm (12.5 in)
This piece is technically excellent, with an interesting but not excessive variety of fillings and a fairly long pattern repeat; but a certain stiffness in the design, regularity of the raised outlining, and comparative coarseness of the thread for the scale of design betray its 19th-century date.

b.   Collar: late 19th C.
   Depth 5.5 cm (2.1 in)
   Overall length 39 cm (15.5 in)
Another technically excellent piece with fine, graduated raised work, but the effect is killed by its brilliant whiteness, produced by modern washing powders or bleach.

c.   Collar: late 19th–20th C.
   Length of neck edge 30 cm (12 in)
   Depth 5.5 cm (2.2 in)
This example is in very coarse thread and a hybrid 19th-century style, vaguely reminiscent of late 17th-century designs when pattern motifs were getting smaller and a coarse mesh ground was developing.

d.   Table mat: about 1975.
   Length 24.5 cm (9.7 in)
   Depth 14.5 cm (5.7 in)
This was bought new. The coarse brides, rigid outlining and formalization of design are typical of needlepoint lace made this century for household use. It is probably of Chinese manufacture.

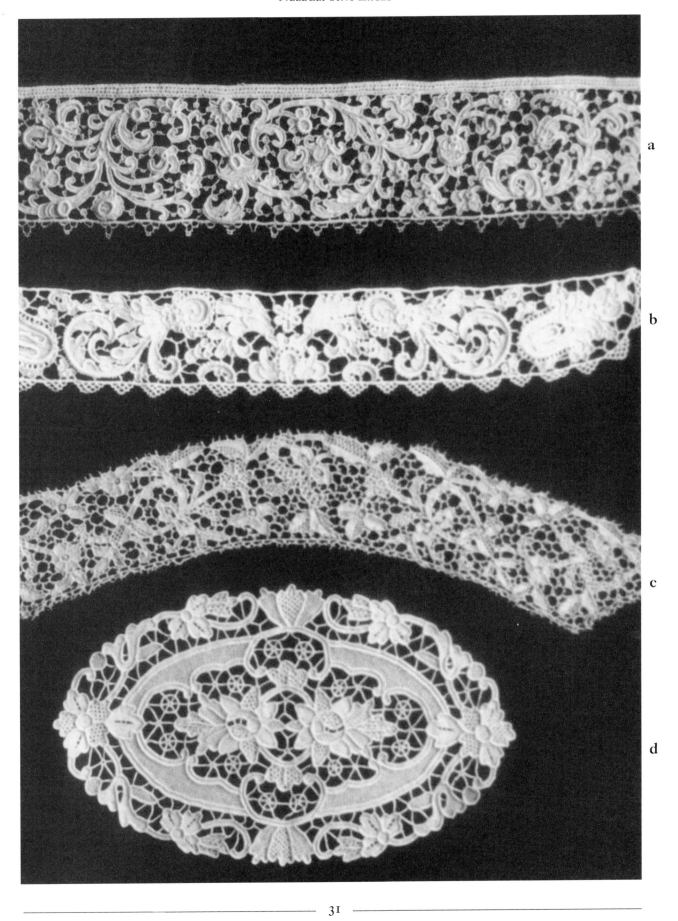

a

b

c

d

FRENCH NEEDLEPOINTS

POINT DE FRANCE

Characteristics
1. Guipure needlepoint lace.
2. Mainly flat but with some pronounced foundation threads within the design and padded curves closely-covered with buttonhole stitches on the surface.
3. Designs include narrow bands of clothwork; these may form branching patterns in the late 17th-century Italian baroque style (Plate 23a) or may outline pattern areas worked in more open stitches.
4. Ground of interconnected, buttonholed brides with added picots forming irregular meshes.
5. Frequent use of bars or outlines based on a thick foundation thread with loosely-worked buttonhole stitches forming a row of loops on one or each side.

Points to watch
Point de France is a late 17th- to early 18th-century lace which initially copied Venetian needlepoints and can be confused with them (see pages 26–31). Apart from stylistic factors, points to look for are the closeness of Italian working, with fillings constituted by arrays of holes in the clothwork, compared with the looser, more open French work.

Brussels also made needlepoint guipures in the French manner (Plate 37a) but the treatment of the work was even lighter than the French. It is now thought that many early 18th-century flounces which had been attributed to Sedan in Northern France were probably made in Brussels.

History
The French lace industry did not develop in commercial terms until the 1660s, the time of Colbert, Louis XIV's great finance minister. Realizing that imports of foreign luxury goods were damaging the economy, he persuaded lace makers from Venice and Flanders to settle in France to improve the quality of the local products. The Venetian workers were brought to Colbert's château at Alençon where, after a difficult beginning, successful imitations of the Venetian rose points were made. These, and the bobbin laces, were initially sold as 'Point de France' and gained acceptance both at the French court and abroad.

By the 1670s new styles were being sought and it was probably the influence of government-paid designers, firstly Le Brun and later Bérain, who caused the introduction of

PLATE 22: **Detail of Plate 21 showing: narrow bands of clothwork surrounding areas of filling stitches; picoted brides connected into large-scale, irregular meshes; and a raised detail.**

the lighter, classical designs usually associated with the French needlepoints of this period. In these, individual motifs still have a curving baroque appearance but are separated from each other and grouped about vertical axes. Human figures, classical ornaments and architectural features add a touch of life while the small scale of the motifs requires the use of a multitude of connecting brides, now organized into irregular meshes.

This light but all-over patterning suited the tastes of the late 17th century but fashion never stays still. In the early 18th century the trend was again towards fuller designs and the motifs, which had been small and slender, expanded to fill space previously occupied by the mesh ground. In the larger, furnishing flounces, many designs continued to be based on axes of symmetry, but a new baroque influence was being felt: this will be seen more clearly in the bobbin-lace chapters.

By the 1730s, the guipure needlepoints were giving way to the mesh-grounded forms of 'Alençon' and 'Argentan' described in the next section.

PLATE 21: **Part of a flounce of point de France: about 1700–20.**
The complete flounce is several metres long and over $\frac{1}{2}$ metre deep and is typical of the furnishing flounces produced in the early 18th century. The motifs are larger and less attenuated, the design more crowded than in 17th-century examples.

Private collection

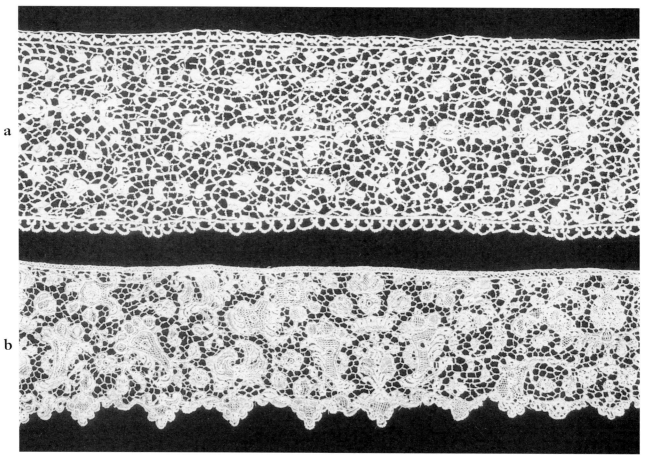

PLATE 23:
a.   Edging: about 1700.
      Depth 10 cm (4.0 in)
This design, or rather lack of it, is more typical of Venetian work
of the period but the looser working, use of bars with loops along
each side (see point 5 above) and symmetry of the motifs, indicate
a French origin.

b.   Edging: about 1700.
      Depth 7.5 cm (3.0 in)
      Length shown 32 cm (12.5 in); design incomplete
This is not of the highest quality expected of point de France and
could perhaps be Brussels work; Plate 37a shows an example more
certainly attributable to Brussels. The design has been altered at a
later date.

FIGURE 4: Woman's fontange head-dress; 1690–1700.
A curious feature of the 1690s was the woman's towering head-
dress, a pleated frill up to 30 cm (1 ft) high, wired to stand up from
a small cap. Lappets, or streamers, which hung from the back of
the cap, were also introduced at about this time. They were to gain
more importance in the 18th century (see Figure 6).

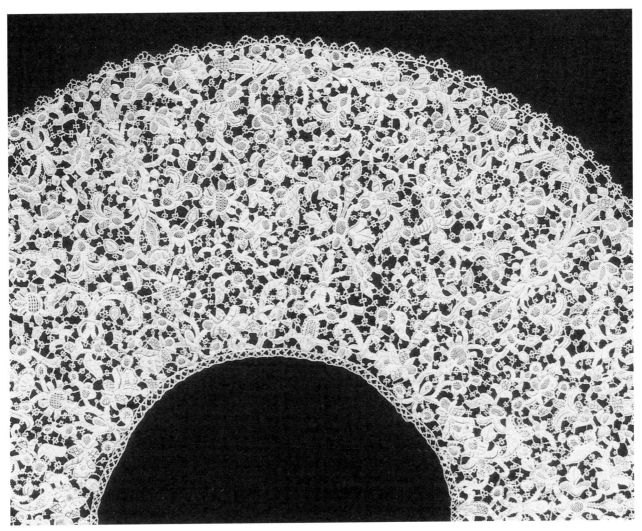

PLATE 24: **Part of a needlepoint bertha collar: about 1890–1900.**
  Depth of lace 18.5 cm (7.2 in)
  Diameter of neck opening 20 cm (8 in)
The complete bertha occupies one and a half circles.
  Circular bertha collars are typical of the late 19th to early 20th
centuries and, in this case, would probably have been worn
gathered over the full sleeves of the mid-1890s. The design is a
hybrid of the repeated, symmetrical groups of point de France,
here arranged around radii of the circle, and the decorated brides
and raised work of Venetian needlepoints of about 1700.

Characteristics

1. Needlepoint laces incorporating one or more of the grounds explained below.
2. Raised outline to the design formed by surface threads closely covered in buttonhole stitches and sometimes decorated with picots; called the 'cordonnet'.
3. Pattern areas filled with closely packed buttonhole stitches.
4. Areas of filling stitches common, particularly combinations of tightly buttonholed rings, stars and bars with open stitches on each side.
5. Grounds:

    a. Alençon (Figure 5)
    Roughly hexagonal mesh with two threads twisted together on each side. (This is formed by linked rows of loose buttonhole stitches usually worked at right-angles to the length of the lace; each new row is looped into the previous row and a strengthening thread is run back through this row before the next is started. The strengthening thread is not tightened, allowing the meshes to retain a hexagonal shape.)

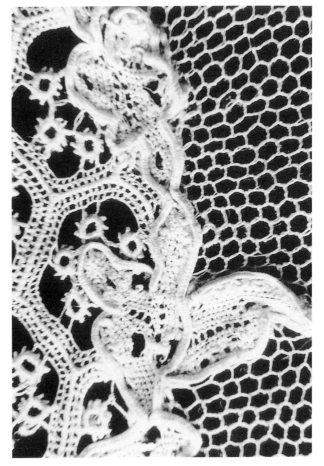

PLATE 26: Detail of a French needlepoint edging showing the Alençon ground, the raised, closely buttonholed outline, or cordonnet, and filling stitches.

PLATE 25: Sleeve ruffle and matching edging with the Alençon ground in the major area and the Argentan ground in the border: about 1760–75.

    Maximum depth of ruffle 14.5 cm (5.6 in)
    Minimum depth of ruffle 7.0 cm (2.7 in)
    Length of outer edge 106 cm (42 in)
    Depth of edging 5.5 cm (2.3 in)
    Pattern repeat 20 cm (8 in)

Until the end of the 18th century, women's sleeve ruffles were attached to the chemise rather than to the dress and were worn above or below the elbow according to the decade. When shaped, as in the example shown, the wider part fell behind the elbow. Ruffles were often made in sets in graduated sizes, and with a matching cap back, lappets (see Figure 6, page 40), and narrower and wider edgings for the cap frill and dress trimmings.

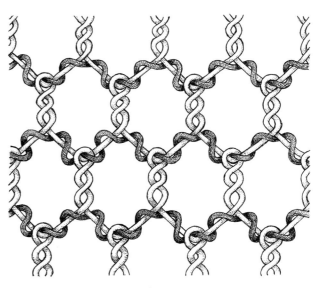

FIGURE 5: The Alençon ground.

b. Argentan (Plate 27)
Hexagonal mesh of larger scale than the Alençon mesh, with close buttonhole stitches worked over the foundation threads on all six sides.

c. Tortillée (Plate 28)
A hexagonal mesh with each side reinforced by an additional thread twisted, or formed into widely spaced buttonhole stitches, around it, giving an untidy appearance when magnified.

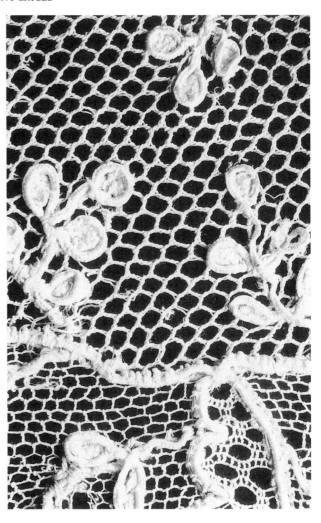

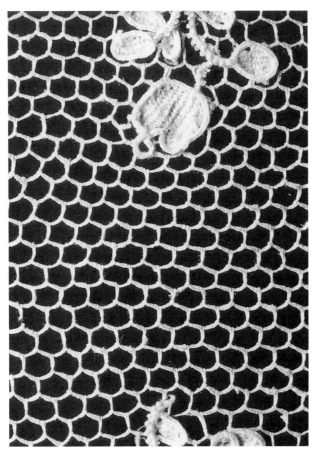

PLATE 27: **Detail of the Argentan ground.**

PLATE 28: **Detail of the edging in Plate 30***b***, showing the Alençon ground, the tortillée ground and plain and picoted raised work.**

Points to watch

Burano laces (pages 44–5) use a ground very similar to the Alençon ground but the Burano ground often has a ladder-like appearance and the Burano raised work is not closely buttonholed. French needlepoints with damaged grounds were often regrounded in Burano in the 19th century.

To the naked eye, well-made Alençon grounds look like the simplest of the bobbin-made nets, Lille or East Midlands point ground. A magnifying glass, however, will show the looped buttonhole stitches.

The Alençon ground was sometimes used for part bobbin laces and tape laces in the 19th century.

PLATE 29: **Group of French needlepoint edgings.**
   Maximum length shown 37 cm (14.5 in)

a and b.   Two fragments from the same design with the Alençon ground: about 1730–40. Design incomplete.
   Maximum depth 7 cm (2.4 in)

c.   Alençon ground: about 1760–70; design altered.
   Depth 8 cm (3 in)
This is a typical example of a floral sprig springing from a border pattern and extending asymmetrically in two directions along the lace.

d.   Argentan ground: about 1760–70.
   Depth 5 cm (2 in)
   Pattern repeat 22.5 cm (9 in)
The symmetry of this design shows the influence of classical styles which gradually superseded the rococo in the late 18th century. The bow motif is also common in late 18th-century designs.

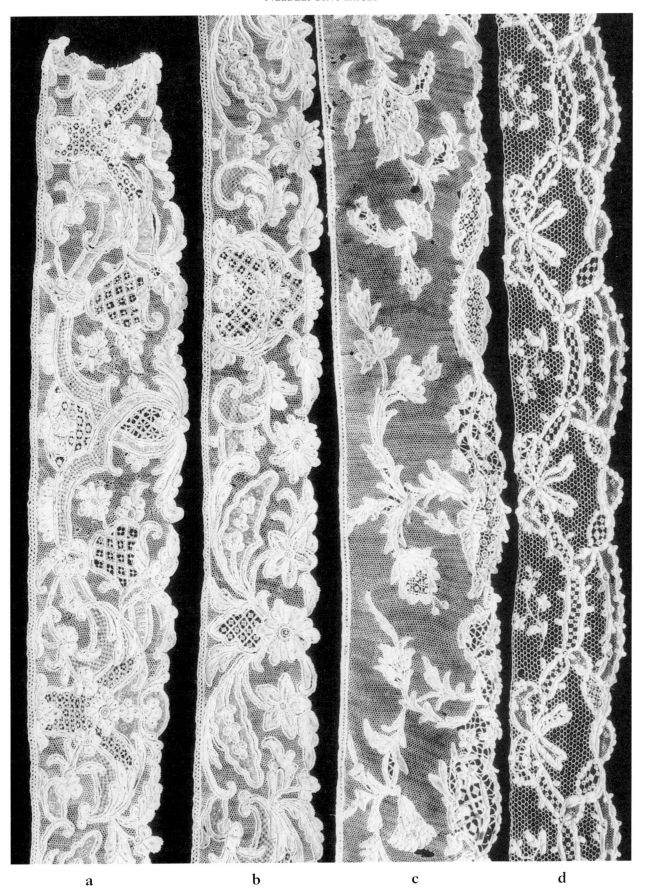

a   b   c   d

History

In the early 18th century the French needlepoint industry, established around Alençon and neighbouring Argentan in Normandy, was in decline. Fashion preferred plain muslins and feather-light bobbin laces to the crisp, heavy texture of needlepoints and point de France was made largely for household use, in wide flounces suitable for masking baths and dressing tables.

It was not until the 1730s that needlepoints were again made in any quantity for dress trimmings. By this time the coarse, picoted meshes of point de France had given way to much finer meshes of regular, buttonholed hexagons and an alternative, lighter mesh of open buttonhole stitches had developed: these grounds came to be known as the Argentan and Alençon grounds respectively although each was worked in both towns and they are often found in the same lace. The raised outline typical of Alençon and Argentan work had also become common although it was not so stiff, nor so heavily decorated with picots as it later became.

These changes in technique were accompanied by changes in design. In the earlier years of the century, the more fashionable Flemish bobbin laces had been transformed by the introduction of the so-called 'bizarre' designs (see pages 107–111 and Plates 97a, 111a and 123a). These were also introduced into the French needlepoints but with less success. The movement of the design which should flow from edge to edge is often arrested by symmetrical groupings retained from the earlier French style; the odd lozenge and cartouche shapes filled with fancy stitches appear as clumsy insertions rather than integral parts of the design; and the leaf sprays which should be light and feathery are solid in outline and mixed with poorly drawn flowers.

By the 1740s, designs had opened out from the dense, baroque patterning of the bizarre to the light-heartedness of the rococo. Bands of foliage and cartouches still swept from edge to edge but were more finely drawn and crossed in the centre to define open spaces. Into these burst asymmetric floral sprays, first from one side, then the other.

The trend towards lightness and openness of design continued. In the second half of the century, the bands of foliage and cartouches were largely confined to the edges of the lace. Floral sprays still burst from the borders but then spread along the length of the pattern as they were freed from confinement in enclosed spaces. Gradually they became thinner and weaker or broke entirely from the rest of the design. Occasionally in lace of the 1760s and 1770s, ribbons or narrow stems carrying tiny leaves and flowers meander along the centre or edge of the design, or again cross from side to side.

As the 18th century drew to a close, the scale of the motifs grew smaller as it had in the late 17th century but the all-over patterning was not repeated. Instead, the sprigs and flowerheads were arranged along the edges of wide borders of net ground sprinkled with even tinier flowers and spots.

The general desire at this period for light laces which would gather into soft frills led to a discarding of the stiffer Argentan ground in favour of the tortillée which was quicker and easier to make, particularly in fine meshes. Surprisingly this was also the period when the buttonholed outlines of French needlepoints became stiffest and heaviest: both the outline itself and the picots which stand out from it like rows of bristles were often worked over horsehair and, although this should have been removed from the picots, it can still sometimes be seen.

Until the 1790s, the French needlepoint industry was fortunate in that, despite the underlying trend in fashion towards lighter fabrics which led to a decline in many areas of the lace industry, it supplied a product which was *de rigueur* at the French court in winter. With the Revolution,

FIGURE 6: Woman's dress in the mid-18th century.
In about 1700 the towering frill of the fontange head-dress (Figure 4) started to point forwards and grew smaller. By the 1720s it had become a small frill gathered around the front and sides of a roughly semi-circular cap: this form was retained for formal wear for the next 50 years although close-fitting caps or bonnets were worn on less formal occasions.

A pair of streamers, called lappets, were also part of formal wear. These hung down from the back of the cap and their length and the way they were worn, whether pinned up or hanging free, was governed by strict rules of etiquette.

this came to an end. Many of the French lace makers are reputed to have fled the country or to have gone to the guillotine because their craft was associated with the aristocracy and even Napoleon's attempts to revive the industry in the early 19th century met with little success.

Until fashions changed the needle-lace makers were forced to turn their skills to embroidering muslins and machine-made nets. It was not until the mid-19th century that the rich, floral designs, to which French needlepoints were particularly suited, returned.

The later 19th century was a difficult period for the lace industry in general because of competition from machine-made products. The French needlepoint industry continued thanks to the vigour and enthusiasm of manufacturers like Lefébure at Bayeux, who took great pains to supply good patterns to his workers and demand the highest standards of workmanship. The result was an extremely handsome and expensive product aimed largely at the top end of the market, with the most extravagant pieces being made for exhibition.

By the end of the century, the wheel of fashion had turned full circle and the designs of the late 18th century were being repeated, usually in a stiff mechanical manner. This was to be the end of the industry, as such. Although small amounts of lace continue to be made at Argentan and at the re-opened lace school in Alençon, it is too time-consuming a product to be economic in the 20th century.

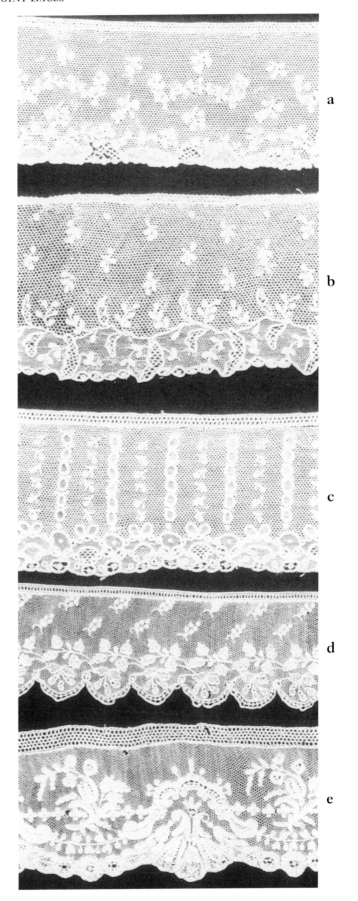

PLATE 30: **Group of French needlepoint edgings: length shown 14.5 cm (5.7 in).**

a. **With tortillée ground: about 1780–95.**
    Depth 7 cm (2.7 in)
    Pattern repeat 14.5 cm (5.7 in)

b. **With tortillée ground: about 1780–1800.**
    Depth 9 cm (3.5 in)
    Pattern repeat 4 cm (1.6 in)
    (See Plate 28 for detail.)

c. **With tortillée ground: about 1785–1810.**
    Depth 8 cm (3.0 in)
    Pattern repeat 2.5 cm (1 in)

d. **With Alençon ground: 1825–40.**
    Maximum depth 5 cm (2 in)
    Pattern repeat 2 cm (1 in)
This shows a stage in the development of design in the 19th century from the straight-edged borders of about 1800, with simple, repeated flowerheads to slightly more elaborate floral patterns.

e. **With Alençon ground: about 1845–60.**
    Depth 7.5 cm (3 in)
    Pattern repeat 10 cm (4 in)
All the edgings in this plate include a later machine- or bobbin-made footing which is included in the depth measurement.

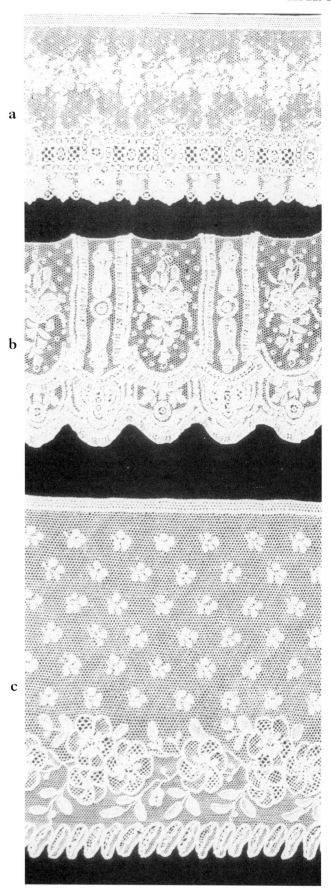

PLATE 31: In all these 19th-century edgings the clothwork is much less closely worked than in the 18th-century examples: length shown 15 cm (6 in).

a. With Alençon ground: 1850–75.
   Depth (including footing) 9 cm (3.5 in)
   Pattern repeat 3.5 cm (1.3 in)

b. With Alençon ground: 1860–80.
   Maximum depth 10 cm (4 in)
   Pattern repeat 2.3 cm (1.3 in)

c. With tortillée ground: 1880–1900, in early 19th C style.
   Depth 17 cm (6.7 in)
   Pattern repeat 8.5 cm (3.4 in)

MESH-GROUNDED FLAT POINT
– VENETIAN?

Characteristics

1. Flat needlepoint lace with mesh ground.

2. Pattern areas of closely-packed buttonhole stitches often enlivened with arrangements of holes.

3. The thick foundation thread outlining the pattern is barely noticeable.

4. Open filling stitches are used as well as arrays of holes in the clothwork.

5. Ground (see Figure 7, page 45): generally-rectangular meshes formed by rows of loose buttonhole stitches worked into previous rows with a strengthening thread along each row. The rows usually extend parallel to the length of the lace not perpendicular to it as in Burano laces.

PLATE 32:

a. Edging: 1720–40; design incomplete and altered.
    Maximum depth 5.5 cm (2.2 in)
    Length shown 26 cm (10 in)

b. Edging: late 18th C; 1760–75. Design incomplete.
    Maximum depth 4.7 cm (1.8 in).

Flat needlepoints with mesh grounds were made in various parts of Europe in the 18th century and are not easy to distinguish from each other. Some were made in coarse thread, in scrolling tape designs derived from Italian bobbin laces (see Plates 79c and 81): these often have irregular grounds worked in different directions within the same lace, and many are attributable to Austria and Germany. Others, like the edging shown below, were worked in finer thread, in designs more acceptable to fashionable society. The finest of these were probably made in Brussels. A superb example is illustrated in *Lace: A History*, by S. Levey (Maney & Son, 1983).

The above characteristics are based on the intermediate-quality edgings shown below. Unfortunately most of them also apply to Brussels flat points. It is only fine details of technique and texture that suggest that, wherever these edgings were made, it was not Brussels.

In the past, laces of this type have been attributed to Venice but this origin is by no means certain. It is perhaps supported by the similarity of their ground to that of later Burano laces (pages 44–45) and the fact that many of the filling stitches in the earlier examples are formed in the Venetian manner, by arrays of holes in the clothwork.

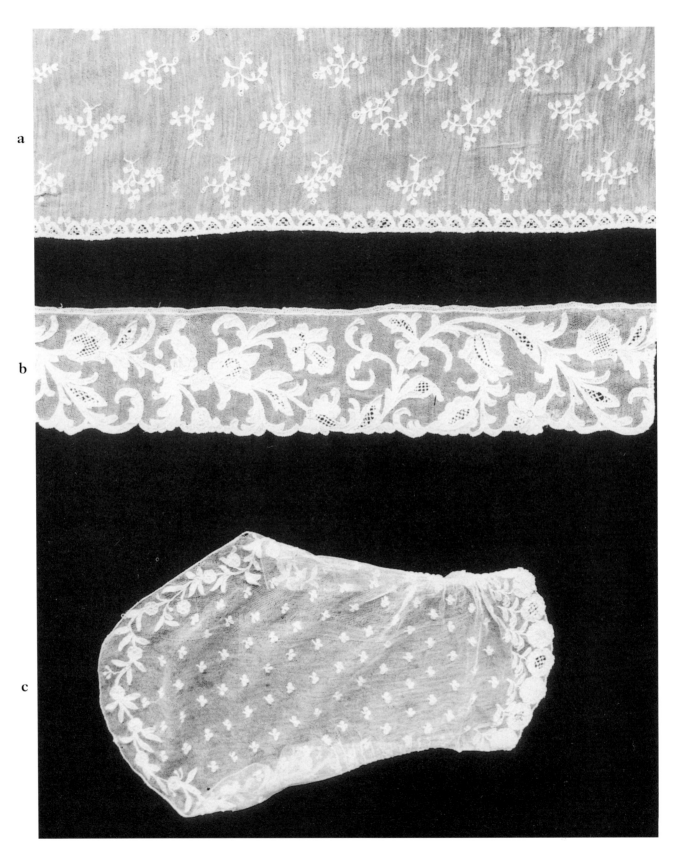

a

b

c

Characteristics

1. Needlepoint lace with net ground.
2. Raised outline to the design formed by surface threads sewn with overcast stitches.
3. Pattern areas often have a ribbed appearance.
4. A slightly fuzzy appearance is common, particularly in the ground, due to the poor-quality thread often used.
5. Ground (Figure 7): generally-rectangular meshes with two threads twisted on each side, arranged in rows perpendicular to the length of the lace. The net is formed by linked rows of loose buttonhole stitches with a strengthening thread along each row. This is pulled taut to give a ladder-like appearance, unlike the Alençon ground.

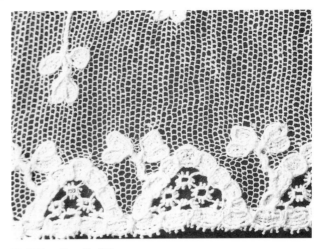

PLATE 34: **Detail of Plate 33***a*.

FIGURE 7: **The Burano ground.**

PLATE 33:
a. Flounce: 1800–10.
    Depth 18 cm (7 in)   Depth shown 16 cm (6.2 in)
    Pattern repeat 15 cm (6 in)
Note the cloudy, ladder-like appearance of the ground, typical of Burano work.

b. Edging: late 19th C.
    Depth 9.5 cm (3.7 in)
    Pattern repeat 41 cm (16 in)
    Length shown 50 cm (19.5 in)
This style of design, reminiscent of the late 17th century but with a distinctly later use of fillings and of the mesh ground, is characteristic of one type of Burano lace.

c. Sleeve: early 20th C: about 1910
    Maximum length 38 cm (15 in)
The stiffness of the design and feel of this piece would betray its date if it had not been obvious from the sleeve shape. The row of flower heads along the edge is copied from early 19th-century designs.

Points to watch

See Alençon and Argentan laces. The rectangular Burano mesh distinguishes it from the structurally similar, but hexagonal, Alençon mesh. The tightly buttonholed French outline is also distinctive.

History

Burano is one of the islands in the Venetian Lagoon and presumably its populace contributed to the extensive Venetian needlepoint industry in the 17th century. The collapse of this industry in the early 18th century was almost total but some lace continued to be made, possibly including the type illustrated on page 43.

The extent of the Burano industry in the late 18th and early 19th centuries is unclear but, in 1872, it had almost completely died out when a particularly hard winter and famine brought about the establishment of a lace school. At first, early 19th-century Alençon laces were copied, but in the rather quicker technique which came to characterize Burano work. Soon the industry was thriving again with lace being made in almost every style imaginable from close copies of 17th-century Venetian rose points and fine mid-18th-century French laces to derivatives such as that shown in Plate 24.

Although demand for costume lace diminished in the 1910s, the Burano industry continued by making guipures for household linen. When increasing labour costs made this uneconomic, the market was left mainly to Far Eastern competitors whose imports continue to be sold as 'Venetian' or 'Renaissance' lace (Plate 20*d*).

It is pleasing to note that the recent revival of interest in lace and lace-making has led to the re-opening of the Burano school.

BRUSSELS NEEDLEPOINTS

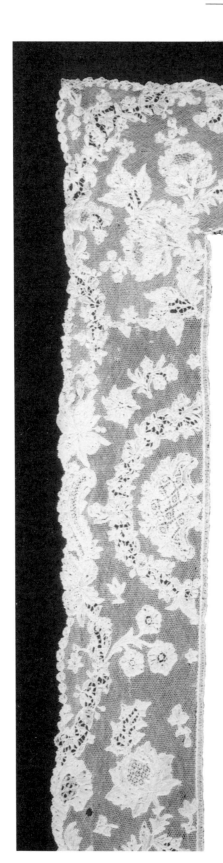

PLATE 35: Edging, possibly from a kerchief: about 1755–75.
　Depth of edging 7.5 cm (3 in)
　Length of free vertical edge shown 37 cm (14.5 in)
　Overall length of edge 84 cm (33 in)
　(The two edges are of the same length and square ended.)
The needlepoint pattern motifs are joined by bobbin-made
drochel ground. The naturalistically drawn flowers and leaves are
typical of Brussels designs.

Characteristics

1.　Needlepoint lace with various grounds.
2.　Raised outlines to the design formed by bundles of
threads on the surface caught by loosely spaced buttonhole
stitches, except in early examples.
3.　Pattern areas filled with loosely packed buttonhole
stitches.
4.　Areas of filling stitches common.
5.　Grounds:
　　a.　Buttonholed brides decorated with picots and
　　sometimes arranged in irregular meshes (used in the
　　very early 18th century – Plate 37a).
　　b.　Loosely-worked buttonhole stitches forming large-
　　scale meshes between nearly touching pattern parts
　　(Plate 36b).
　　c.　Alençon-type needle ground (Figure 5 – early-mid-
　　18th century).
　　d.　Brussels vrai drochel bobbin ground (Figure 8).
　　Hexagonal mesh with two sides of four plaited threads
　　and four sides of two twisted threads (commonly used
　　from the mid-18th to mid-19th centuries).
　　e.　Machine net (see pages 50–1 – used from the early
　　19th century onwards).
　　f.　Point de gaze needlepoint ground (see pages 52–3 –
　　used from the mid-19th century onwards).

Points to watch

The early guipure needlepoint (Plate 37a) can be confused with point de France although its construction is generally looser than French work. A flat needle lace with a mesh ground similar to the Alençon ground was also made in Brussels in the 18th century – see page 43.

History

Although Brussels lies in the province of Brabant, the history of its laces is so closely linked with that of neighbouring Flanders that we can no longer distinguish Brussels laces from those made in the Flemish towns in the 17th century. Only at the very end of the century did distinctions arise, both in the bobbin laces and in the needlepoints of these regions.

At this time France, under Louis XIV, was arguably the most powerful country in Europe and dominated the fashionable scene. The classical style of point de France (Plate 21), with its underlay of baroque ornamentation, was adopted in Brussels and it is only the looser working of Brussels needlepoints, and perhaps their rather less assured designs, that enable us to identify the Brussels pieces.

As the lace trade picked up after the decline at the beginning of the 18th century, the styles of Brussels and French needlepoints diverged. The softer, more popular Brussels bobbin laces had developed feathery leaf patterns which were followed in some of her needlepoints while the rich texture of the 'bizarre' patterns introduced in the 1710s led to an increased use of fancy filling stitches.

Other changes were inevitable. The closely spaced motifs of the 'bizarre' period had little need for connecting brides and these were replaced by loose buttonhole stitches, sometimes forming large, open meshes. Where the larger scale of a design left wider spaces, and in the later less crowded laces of the rococo period, a net ground similar to that of Alençon (Figure 5, page 37) was adopted.

By the mid-18th century fashion preferred more open designs set off against clear spaces. Brussels was well placed to cater for this taste; its bobbin-lace makers had developed the gossamer-light drochel net and this was now used to ground its needlepoints. At first it was worked into the edges of the needle-made motifs which were arranged face down on a pattern; the threads of this bobbin ground can often be seen crossing loosely over the backs of the motifs from one area of working to the next. Later, as the size of the motifs diminished, it was quicker to make the ground in complete panels and then to apply the motifs to it. This is the technique used in the fichu in Plate 38.

It is apparent from Plate 38 that Brussels could and did meet the demands of the late 18th century for fabrics lightly patterned with classical designs. However, these fashions were met equally well, and more cheaply, by fine muslins and gauzes, and by the lighter forms of bobbin lace. The resulting decline in the Brussels industry was aggravated by the French revolution and subsequent wars with France,

PLATE 36:
(*left*). Detail of Plate 35 showing the looped structure of the needlepoint motifs against the plaited and twisted meshes of the bobbin ground.
(*right*). Detail of the central edging in Plate 37 showing the closely spaced motifs joined by loose buttonhole stitches.

Compare the raised outline of these two examples with that of the French needlepoints in Plate 26.

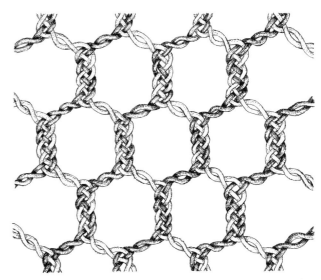

FIGURE 8: The Brussels vrai drochel bobbin ground.

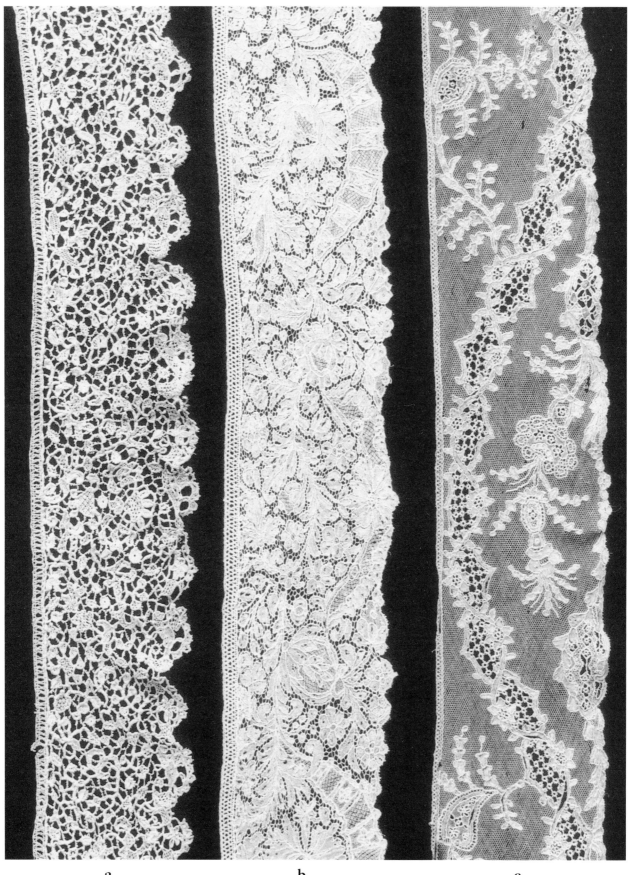

a   b   c

PLATE 38: Fichu or half kerchief of Brussels needlepoint applied to a bobbin drochel ground: about 1800.

Maximum depth 51 cm (20 in)

Maximum length (when flat) 109 cm (43 in)

The ground is made in three panels: a central triangle and two edging strips. Each of these is made up from narrower strips (about 1 cm wide) joined edge to edge. The design is in the classical style fashionable in the late 18th century and early 19th century.

PLATE 37: Group of Brussels needlepoint edgings: length shown 35 cm (13.7 in).

a.   (*left*). With a ground of coarse irregular meshes: about 1700.
Maximum depth 7 cm (2.7 in)

This has a scattering of tiny motifs typical of Venetian laces of about 1700 (see Plate 16) but some are symmetrically grouped as in contemporary point de France lace (see Plates 21 and 23). The scalloped edge is also typical of point de France but the stitching is looser than in French needlepoints.

b.   (*centre*): about 1720–30. (See Plate 36 for detail.)
Depth 7.5 cm (3 in)
Pattern repeat 58 cm (23 in)

c.   Motifs joined by the bobbin drochel ground: about 1760–75.
Depth 7.5 cm (3 in)
Pattern repeat 70 cm (27.5 in)

FIGURE 9: Woman in late 18th-century dress with a half-kerchief. A half-kerchief was a generally triangular piece of material, sometimes of lace, often of embroidered lawn or muslin, which was worn around the neck and shoulders and often tucked into the front of the bodice. The ends of larger examples might be fastened around the waist. A kerchief (square in shape) was usually folded diagonally and worn in the same way.

PLATE 39: **Bonnet veil of Brussels needlepoint applied to machine-made net: about 1840–50.**

> Depth 49 cm (19 in)
> Width shown 61 cm (24 in)
> Full width 124 cm (49 in)

Veils became fashionable in the early 19th century and were particularly popular with the wide-brimmed bonnets of the 1820s and 1830s. During this period they were often a metre or more deep and just as wide. Veils for wear with the later close-fitting bonnets were correspondingly smaller.

Veils which were intended to be worn with a bonnet usually have a casing or a footing with a row of holes to take a drawstring along the upper edge. Most of the pattern is concentrated along the bottom edge but a narrow border usually continues up the two side edges as in this example.

but was not as drastic as in France itself. Even so, the volume of lace produced fell and was not to be restored fully until the mid-19th century.

In the early 19th century, the Brussels workers had one advantage over the French: they were accustomed to applying needlepoint motifs to bobbin-made net. This practice continued but they also transferred the technique to the machine-made nets which, by the 1820s, were widely available. They also quickened their rate of working by reducing the density of the clothwork areas and were thus able to produce fabrics which could compete with the less expensive embroidered nets, muslins and light blonde laces (pages 162–5) which were all the rage at the time.

By 1850 scarcely any bobbin net was being made but a new, lighter needlepoint net had been introduced. This was the point de gaze ground, named for its light, gauzy appearance.

Fashions had again changed by this time. The patterns of tiny flowerheads along the headside of the lace in the early 1800s had developed into curved sprigs by the 1820s but, by

1840, the rococo style of the mid-18th century had returned. Many of the smaller edgings were made in patterns very similar to their earlier counterparts although wider flounces and bonnet veils, such as that in Plate 39, were often made in a lighter floral style. Here the weight of the design is still concentrated near the headside, as it had been for the last 60 to 70 years, but tendrils bearing stylized leaves and flowers stretch tentatively upwards. The scrolls, ribbons and strapwork which were to gain greater importance in the second half of the century are already seen in a narrow, trailing form. The overall feeling is one of lightness and asymmetry.

The 1850s and 1860s saw a gradual development of this style with designs becoming fuller and more assured. The straight or slightly wavy headside of the 1840s gave way to deep scallops filled with massed flowerheads, cartouches or fanned strapwork. The footside, which had been substantially free of pattern became filled with pendant sprays and garlands. These intertwined with richly-patterned strapwork, ribbons and floral swags stretching up from the footside to form frames for elaborate bouquets of flowers.

The whole effect is a fine combination of richness and balance. Individual sprays are rarely symmetrical and asymmetric scrolls often link one pattern repeat to the next but there is no sense of continuous movement; asymmetric flower arrangements are often confined within symmetrical frames and forwardly scrolling motifs in one part of a design are balanced by backward movement in another.

The 1870s saw little change in these designs apart from a certain stiffness and formality creeping in but there was one technical innovation: the introduction of raised petals (Plates 43 and 44). These are worked separately from the rest of the design and sewn on to the surface along one edge to give a three-dimensional, tiered effect. Most commonly they are found on the roses which are almost ubiquitous in Brussels designs but occasionally they are found on other flowers or motifs.

In the 1870s, the Brussels point de gaze industry did not suffer the same decline as other lace industries since its rich flounces and matching trimmings retained considerable popularity for wedding trousseaux. It was no doubt this use that enabled its designs to continue into the 1880s and 1900s, making the dating of point de gaze and associated Brussels bobbin laces extremely difficult.

The 1880s did, however, see the return of the rococo influence. Cartouches, scrolls and shell shapes patterned with filling stitches first became more prominent then, gradually, the flowers and strapwork became weaker and more insipid. By the late 1890s and 1900s the floral swags were often reduced to meandering tendrils and it is sometimes difficult to distinguish laces from this period from those of the 1840s. This is particularly true in the case of the long stoles which had been fashionable in the first half of the 19th century and now returned having been ousted by shawls in the days of the crinoline.

The 1900s brought a brief interest in Art Nouveau designs but the First World War sounded the knell of Brussels needlepoints. The fashions of the 1920s had little place for hand-made lace and the making of point de gaze almost died out.

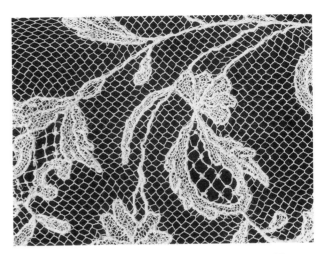

PLATE 40: Detail of the reverse side of the veil in Plate 39. The diamond-shaped meshes of the machine net can be seen across the backs of the clothworked motifs but are cut away behind the open filling stitches. This type of net was first introduced in about 1830.

Note the trailing stems of the flowers formed by bundles of threads like those used to outline the motifs, and the extremely loose working of the buttonholed clothwork which makes the tenuous design even lighter.

The clothwork becomes firmer again in the fuller, more opulent designs of the second half of the century.

BRUSSELS POINT DE GAZE

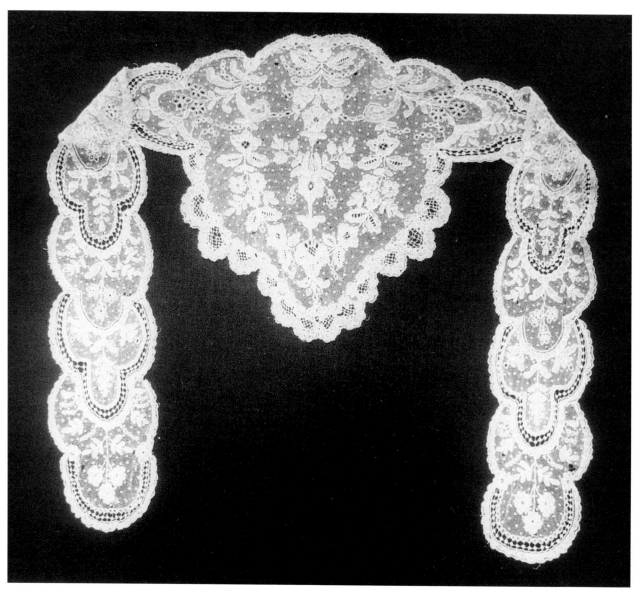

PLATE 41: **Point de gaze fall cap: 1845–60.**
  Depth of centre-piece 24 cm (9.5 in)
  Overall length (unfolded) 109 cm (43 in)
In the 19th century the separate lappets and cap of the 18th
century were largely replaced by fall caps, comprising a pair of
lappets joined by a central cap piece, or by pairs of lappets made
in one piece to go over the head.
  The early fall caps of the 1840s and 50s often had an
asymmetrical centre-piece, with a smaller lobe at the front and a
larger lobe at the back. The centres of later fall caps, from the
1860s to 1880s, tend to be smaller and more symmetrical.
  Note the symmetry in the design, the early, rather tentative use
of strapwork and the spots formed by buttonholed rings scattered
over the ground; spots are typical of 19th-century Brussels laces.

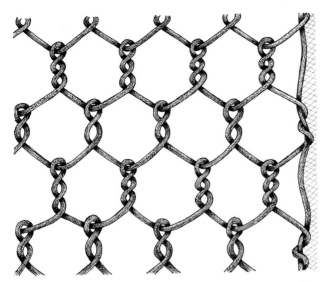

FIGURE 10: The point de gaze ground. Roughly hexagonal mesh with a looped thread twisted on itself on two sides and a single thread on the other sides.

It is formed by linked rows of loosely worked buttonhole stitches which are worked back and forth between the pattern areas. Alternate rows have slightly differing twists.

NOTE: The strengthening thread of the Alençon and Burano grounds is absent.

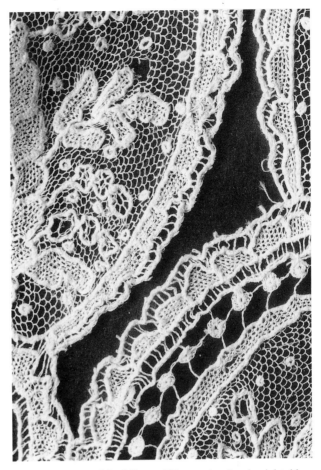

PLATE 42: Detail of the fall cap of Plate 41 showing the right side of the lace on the right and the wrong side on the left.

The bundle of outlining threads loosely caught down by well-spaced buttonhole stitches is seen standing proud on the right side while the wrong side is almost flat. Note the very open clothwork, like that of the veil in Plates 39–40.

FIGURE 11: In the 1840s and 1850s day dresses fitted close around the neck and were often worn with a neat, round collar. To be properly dressed a lady would always have worn some sort of head covering, whether a simple cap in the morning or a more elaborate confection with lace and flowers in the evening.

Notes on point de gaze

The particular characterizing feature of point de gaze lace is its ground, whose light, gauzy appearances gives the lace its name (see Figure 10). In other respects, point de gaze is technically similar to earlier Brussels needlepoints, but its clothwork pattern areas are more loosely worked than in 18th-century laces and its raised outline is more pronounced. Further innovations in the 1870s were the creation of

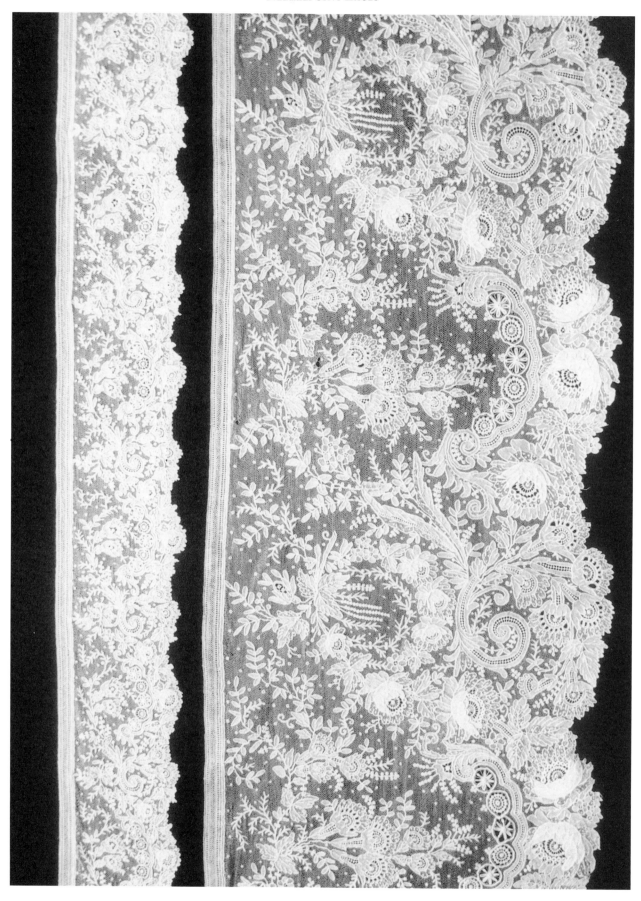

PLATE 44: Detail of Plate 43 showing the tiered petals of rose point de gaze; these are attached to the lace around their outer edges but are free at their scalloped, inner edges.

These three-dimensional petals increase the sense of naturalism in the design, an effect much sought after in the second half of the 19th century. This naturalism is also achieved by the use of denser and less-dense stitching in the clothwork of the motifs to give the effect of shading.

Note also the use of buttonholed rings, as elements of the design, as part of the filling stitches and as spots on the point de gaze ground.

PLATE 43: Flounce and matching edging of rose point de gaze: about 1870–90.

    Flounce-depth 28 cm (11 in)
    Pattern repeat 30 cm (12 in)
    Edging-depth 9 cm (3.5 in)
    Length shown 48 cm (19 in)

The beautifully organized floral design of the flounce, with its garlands and flower sprays, filling the entire panel but giving an impression of opulence rather than overcrowding, is typical of the finer laces of the second half of the 19th century.

These pieces belong to a set, or parure, of lace which was said to be part of a wedding trousseau and consists of: two flounces of the design shown, 240 cm (8 ft) amd 300 cm (10 ft) long respectively; one matching edging (shown); one pair of cuffs made up from another length of the above edging; one pair of full length, close-fitting sleeves; and a sample of the flounce, comprising $1\frac{1}{2}$ pattern repeats.

shading in the pattern motifs by the use of different densities of stitching in adjacent areas and the addition of raised petals (see Plates 43 and 44): this gives the form known as rose point de gaze, or simply Brussels rose point. Here 'rose' is used in the sense of 'raised' as in the earlier Venetian laces.

Point de gaze was made in huge quantities and in large pieces, such as flounces and shawls. To enable these to be worked, the designs were divided into small areas each of which was accomplished by a single lace-maker. The completed parts were then assembled on a master pattern and joined invisibly together. This way, only a small number of workers had access to the overall design which lessened the risk of pirating; lace designing was a very skilled and highly paid job on the continent. The Brussels practice differed from that in France, where each lace-maker specialized in her own task and a pattern piece was passed from hand to hand, the first worker couching the outlining thread, another working the clothwork and others completing the ground and filling stitches. As many as 20 people might thus be employed from the start to the finish of a small piece. It is not certain when this practice developed but it was current by the late 18th century.

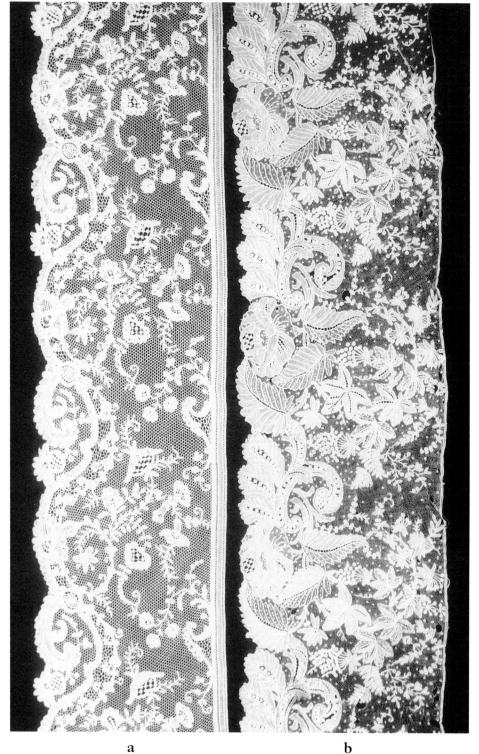

a

b

PLATE 45:

a. Flounce of point de gaze: probably about 1850–70.

Depth 18 cm (7 in)

Pattern repeat 18.5 cm (7.2 in) Although the asymmetry of the repeated motifs gives this design a sense of movement more typical of the late 19th century, the large scale of the design elements suggests an earlier date. The complex filling stitches seen in flounce (*b*) below and in the flounce in Plate 43 are also lacking which reinforces the dating.

b. Flounce of Brussels needlepoint: about 1900.

Depth 17.5 cm (7 in)

Pattern repeat 19.5 cm (7.6 in) This shows the much lighter designs typical of the late 19th to early 20th centuries. The flowers are less naturalistically drawn and carried on curving, tendril-like stems. They are also more widely spaced than in the 1860s and 1870s, but the greater use of filling stitches distinguishes this design from those of the 1840s.

The ground is a hand-made needlepoint ground but much coarser than the point de gaze net.

HOLLIE POINT (ENGLAND)

Characteristics
1. Flat needlepoint lace made with rows of knotted buttonhole stitches worked over stretched threads.
2. Simple designs created by holes left in the otherwise plain clothwork formed by the buttonhole stitches.
3. Found as insertions in babies' clothes from the early 18th to the early 19th centuries, particularly in caps, in the shoulder seams of shirts and in the bibs and detachable sleeves worn over babies' swaddling bands.

History
Hollie point is a peculiarly English lace. The knotted buttonhole stitch differentiates it from continental needlepoints and is found in English needleworks, such as samplers, stumpwork embroideries and tape laces from the second half of the 17th century. Its use in the form known as 'hollie point', with its distinctive delineation of design by means of holes in the clothwork, appears to date from the early 18th century.

The age of hollie point is difficult to determine because of its use of rather naïve, unconnected design motifs, such as birds, flowers and coronets. Only a study of babies' wear can assist.

In general, early 18th-century bonnets tend to be plain apart from a circular or keyhole-shaped insertion of lace in

PLATE 46: Baby's bonnet with hollie point insertion: 1800–25.
Diameter of hollie point 4 cm (1.5 in)
The bonnet is of plain lawn gathered in to the hollie-point cap back and decorated with radiating lines of pulled-thread work. The buttonholed loops which stand proud of the surface are a common decorative feature in 18th-century bonnets; here they show how tradition preserves old design features. The bonnet is too large for a new-born baby and probably was not intended for a christening.

the back and perhaps a lace frill around the brim. The second half of the century saw the introduction of a band of lace extending from the centre front of the bonnet to the nape of the neck, sometimes with a circle in the back. This band was later accompanied by parallel lines of pulled-thread embroidery while, in the early 19th century, the circular cap back reappeared.

In trying to date babies' wear, it must be remembered that items decorated with hollie point were often made for christenings and were surrounded by tradition so that older styles might persist long after they had died out in everyday use. It is also probable that much hollie point was made by the ladies of a household or the nanny rather than by professionals.

YOUGHAL (IRELAND)

PLATE 47: Plastron and collar of Youghal needlepoint: 1885–1900.
  Overall depth 55.5 cm (22 in)
  Overall width 30 cm (12 in)
The plastron was a decorative front sometimes worn over the high-necked bodices of the late 19th and early 20th centuries. This example has the long-waisted look of the 1880s and 1890s. The revived-rococo design of asymmetric floral sprays interlinked by cartouches of fancy fillings is also typical of the period. Unusually for an Irish lace, there are no shamrocks in the design.

Characteristics

1. Flat needlepoint lace.
2. Buttonholed loops, often with scallops of additional buttonhole stitches, surround many motifs within the designs as well as the entire outline of the article, outside the thick foundation threads which are slightly proud on the right side.
3. Pattern of buttonholed clothwork and open areas of linked rows of untwisted loops.
4. Fancy fillings common.
5. Ground of curved, interlinked, picoted brides forming large-scale, irregular meshes. Other large-scale mesh grounds were also used.
6. Sometimes made in cotton but usually in linen thread of good quality though coarse by continental standards.

History

Although some lace was made in Ireland in the 18th century, it was not truly a lace-making country until the mid-19th century when various crafts were introduced, or promoted, to provide the employment desperately needed after the failure of the potato harvests in the 1840s. The making of needlepoint lace was started in several centres. In Youghal, Mother Mary Ann Smith of the Presentation Convent is said to have unpicked a piece of antique Venetian lace to learn the technique, and in 1852 a school was opened to teach local children the craft. The venture was so successful that copies of Venetian needlepoints were soon being made both there and in other centres.

In the 1870s, Youghal suffered the decline which occurred in many similarly situated industries. The initial impetus gave way to stagnation as the same designs were repeated and the lack of tight control over workmanship led to a drop in standards. In many places this was aggravated by the death or departure of the founder of what was, after all, a charitable movement, often reliant on the endeavours of a single person or group of persons to organize manufacture and promote sales.

The 1880s saw a drive throughout Ireland to improve the standards of design and technique in its craft industries. It was probably at this time that the distinctive type of Youghal lace described above developed, and the new technique, combined with new designs from a particularly talented member of the convent community, led to a revival which lasted into the early years of this century.

PLATE 48: Detail of Plate 47.
This shows the typical mesh and outlining of Youghal lace. It is interesting to note that the outline is similar to that of Branscombe tape lace (pages 62–3), although there the likeness ends.

II
EMBROIDERIES AND MINOR TECHNIQUES

TAPE LACES WITH NEEDLEPOINT FILLINGS

a

b

Characteristics

1. Pattern of pre-made tapes completed with needlepoint clothwork, fillings and grounds.
2. The tape is puckered or folded around corners and curves in the design.
3. Wide variety of tapes used (see Plate 51e).
4. Grounds:
   Bride and net grounds are found as in true needlepoint laces.

Points to watch

This section is concerned with tape laces made with a tape manufactured as a straight length, usually by machine although, particularly in early examples, it may have been hand-woven, braided or worked with bobbins. In all cases, the tape is of uniform width or varies with very short pattern repeats. This uniformity and the puckering or folding of the tape around corners distinguish this type of tape lace from bobbin tape laces (usually semi-straight laces: see Plates 81, 86 and 87) in which the tape is worked with bobbins on the pattern so that the threads can be turned smoothly around corners. Such bobbin tape laces are usually joined by bobbin-made brides or net but are sometimes connected by needlework.

Technique

Tape laces are made in a very similar manner to the true needlepoints, the difference being that a prefabricated tape is tacked to the pattern to provide the foundation for the work instead of a single thread or pair of threads.

The tape usually outlines the pattern motifs although it can pass through the centre as in the example in Plate 49a. Once the tape is in place, the motifs are filled in with needlepoint stitches and the ground connecting the motifs is worked. When the lace is completed, the tacking stitches are cut to release it from the pattern.

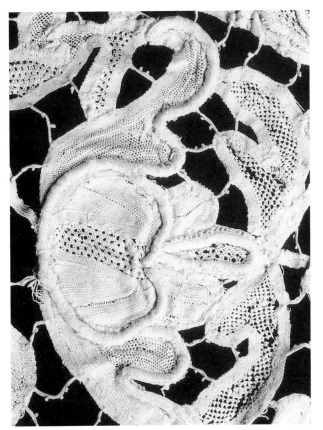

PLATE 50: Detail of the shawl collar in Plate 49b.
The bundle of padding threads in the raised work is visible where the surface buttonhole stitches are worn and broken.

History

In the 16th century, prefabricated tapes and braids in coloured silk and metal threads played an important role in the surface decoration of fabrics. With the growing interest in open, whitework embroidery, the step to incorporate linen tapes in this work was a natural progression. Certainly, by the early 17th century, tape laces were being made in the designs of contemporary punto in aria, designs to which tapes were particularly well suited as will be seen from the example in Plate 12.

Much of the early tape lace was made in Italy, where it was called 'mezzo punto', but the technique spread into other parts of Europe and was found to provide a simple and comparatively quick method of imitating the elaborate Venetian needlepoints of the second half of the 17th century. The lighter laces of the 18th and early 19th centuries did not lend themselves to copying in this way but, when guipure laces returned to fashion in the mid-19th century, tape laces returned with them.

In this later period, much work was done as a craft hobby and patterns were widely available in shops and magazines. Many of the designs were vaguely 17th-century in style and the work was generally known by the fanciful name of 'Renaissance Lace'.

a

b

c

d

e

Compared with true laces, tape work was quick and easy to make and, in a period of competition with machine laces, lace makers in many areas turned to tape laces to earn a living. In England the craft is associated with Branscombe, a small fishing village on the South Devon coast, where Honiton lace had been made until the slump in this trade in the late 1860s to 1870s.

On the continent the work does not appear to have become important industrially until the 1880s or 1890s but has survived in Belgium to the present day in a very coarse form known as 'Luxeuil' in which the tapes are linked by thick threads with little, if any, elaboration by way of fancy fillings.

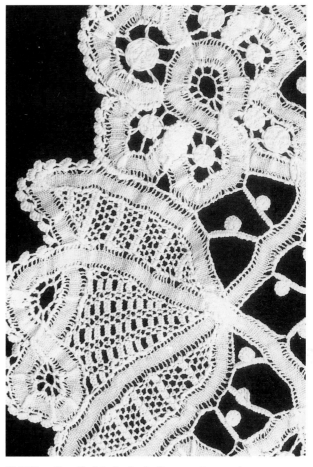

PLATE 51:

a.   **Dress ornament of Branscombe tape lace: probably 1900–20.**
    Depth 11.5 cm (4.5 in)
A detail of Branscombe lace is shown in Plate 52.

b.   **Tape lace edging: late 19th–early 20th C.**
    Depth 5 cm (2 in)
Note the thick thread woven on to the surface of the tape.

c.   **Tape lace collar: 1870–90.**
    Depth 5 cm (2 in)
    Length shown 39 cm (15.5 in)
    Actual length 48 cm (19 in)

d.   **Tape lace edging: late 19th C.**
    Depth 10 cm (4 in)
    Pattern repeat 39 cm (15 in)
A needle-made net ground is less common than bride grounds in tape laces, partly for reasons of fashion, but also because they were slower to make and tape work became popular as a quick and easy form of needlework.

e.   **A group of machine-made tapes which could be used in making a tape lace.**

PLATE 52: Detail of the back of a Branscombe tape-lace mat: early 20th C.
   The edging of tiny buttonholed scallops, the brides decorated with picoted rings, and the variety of fillings, including the needle-woven wheels, are typical of Branscombe work.

AYRSHIRE AND RELATED EMBROIDERY

Characteristics

1.   Whitework embroidery on muslin or cambric.
2.   Satin stitch is used for the majority of the embroidery.
3.   True needlepoint-lace stitches fill openings cut in the muslin or cambric.
4.   Drawn and pulled thread fillings also occur.

PLATE 53: Detail of a handkerchief with whitework embroidery and needlepoint fillings: about 1850–75.
   The same two ovals of filling stitches alternate around the entire periphery of the handkerchief. European, but not Ayrshire. From the collection of Mrs Kathleen Tipping.

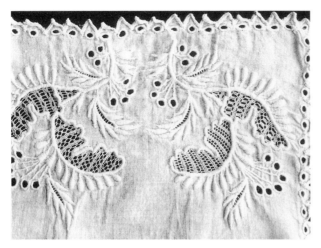

PLATE 54: Detail of Ayrshire whitework embroidery with true needlepoint fillings.

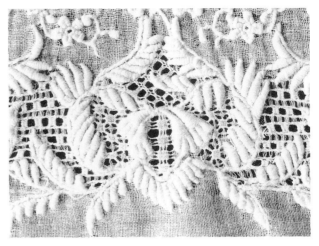

PLATE 55: Detail of whitework embroidery with drawn-thread fillings.

Points to watch

Whitework embroidery was also worked with needlepoint fillings on the continent, particularly in the needle-lace centres of Normandy and Brussels, and in Ireland following the success of the Ayrshire industry. London was also an important centre of whitework embroidery, as was Switzerland. The products of these centres are not clearly distinguishable but Ayrshire work tends to include a wide variety of fillings whereas continental fillings are fewer and more repetitive. Ayrshire work also makes little use of the tightly buttonholed rings and stars which are a legacy of the continental needlepoint industries.

Drawn and pulled thread techniques also create areas of fancy fillings in whitework embroidery and should be distinguished from needlepoint fillings. In both drawn and pulled work, the basic fabric threads can be seen crossing the areas of fancy filling, whereas Ayrshire needlepoint fillings are created in holes cut from the fabric. All three techniques occur in Ayrshire embroideries.

History

Whitework embroidery with needlepoint fillings was introduced into Ayr in the 1820s when the technique is said to have been copied from a French baby robe. The work quickly became popular and was taken up by Glasgow manufacturers as well. Surviving examples show that great care was taken over design and quality of workmanship and it is said that some workers specialized in the embroidery, which was worked first, while more skilled workers completed the filling stitches. The price of a finished article depended on the quantity of filling work in it.

We now associate Ayrshire work with babies' bonnets and long gowns but, in the 1820s to 1840s, Ayrshire supplied the market with many of the dress accessories required at the time. By the 1850s, fashions were turning away from the lighter styles and, although the Ayrshire whitework continued to be made for a decade or so, its market was dwindling and the workers gradually turned to broderie anglaise and other heavier forms of embroidery.

BIBILA AND NETTING

PLATE 56:
a. (*left*). Circular netted mat: 20th C.
  Diameter 18.5 cm (7.2 in)

b. Bag of bibila work lined with pink silk: 1900–10.
  Depth 21 cm (8.5 in)
  Width 15.5 cm (6.2 in)
Art Nouveau designs such as this are not common in lace.

c. Edging of a rectangular tray cloth of bibila work with a green chiffon centre: about 1910–30.
  Width shown 26 cm (10.5 in)
  Full length (not shown) 32 cm (12.5 in)
  Depth of lace 7.5 cm (3 in)
The tray cloth is part of a set with a tea cosy.

PLATE 57: Detail of Plate 56c showing the raised flower petals, a ball worked over a cotton wool core and the bundles of foundation threads within the work.

BIBILA

Characteristics

1. Lace worked with a hooked needle in knotted stitches over stretched foundation threads.
2. Open pattern areas with tiny triangular holes between the stitches and the foundation threads.
3. Designs usually of floral sprays with angular outlines, particularly with diamond-shaped leaves.
4. Ground of curved, interlinked, picoted brides forming large-scale, irregular meshes.

History

Bibila is an Eastern European lace made particularly in Turkey and Greece. In its traditional form, as a decorative edging for scarves, kerchiefs etc., it was usually worked in coloured silks but when it became popular in Western Europe in the late 19th century, goods for export were more often made in white cotton to suit the Western taste.

The main centres of the export industry were Crete and Cyprus. Here goods were made to Western requirements well into the 20th century.

NETTING

Characteristics

1. Knotted net with designs created by variations in the mesh size and shape.
2. Usually found as circular doyleys with the different stitches worked in concentric circles, often with loops, or picots, projecting from the knots into the meshes.

History

Netting is a derivative of filet work (see pages 68–69) but here the pattern is created by variations in the meshes themselves rather than by embroidery on a pre-made net. The technique is somewhat limiting in terms of design but was common as a pastime in the late 18th and 19th centuries and was used for smaller costume accessories, such as gloves and purses, as well as for the ubiquitous doyleys.

SOL OR RUEDAS (SUN OR WHEEL) LACES, INCLUDING TENERIFE AND NANDUTI

Characteristics

1. Needle-woven laces incorporating circular patterns in which foundation threads radiate from a centre, like the spokes of a wheel, and decorated by a thread darned in and out through various combinations of the spokes in ever widening circles.
2. Areas between the circular patterns are often crossed by additional threads also decorated with needle-weaving.
3. a. The original sol work is based on a woven fabric: some threads are pulled out to leave others which are drawn together by the darning thread to form the spoked foundations before the decorative needle-weaving is carried out. It is worked in square or rectangular areas and threads can be seen extending from the woven borders into the sol work.
   b. In the forms known as Tenerife or Nanduti work (see Plate 58b), the needle-weaving is worked on free threads stretched across a pattern.

History

Sol work is a Spanish craft with a long history; examples are known from as early as the 17th century. It was used to decorate domestic linen, both for personal and for household use, and enjoyed a considerable revival in the 19th century when much of the professional work was carried out in the Spanish colonies.

The free form is known either as Tenerife or by its Paraguayan name of Nanduti because of its association with both of these regions. Paraguay has a reputation for the finer work, sometimes in silk, but both regions produced high-quality goods, with complex and varied designs, and the products of the two industries are often indistinguishable.

In simpler work, the decorative wheels are made individually on foundation threads stretched between pins fixed around the periphery of a circle. When completed, the wheels are released from their support and joined together to form larger articles. At first the support was a firmly stuffed cushion but later a metal wheel was invented. More elaborate articles, with complex shapes between the circles, may be worked in one process, directly on the pattern of the finished article.

PLATE 58:
a. Sol work fragment: 19th–20th C.
    Width 23 cm (9 in)
    Depth 12 cm (4.5 in)
Horizontal bands of woven linen with simple pulled-thread work
alternate with bands of the more complex 'sol' work; here, most of
the horizontal fabric threads are removed and the remaining
vertical threads drawn into the sun, or wheel, patterns.

b. Collar of Tenerife or Nanduti work: 1900–20.
    Maximum width 28 cm (11 in)
This shows only a few of the multitude of wheel patterns which
can be made. The needle-weaving of the outer leaves closely
resembles bobbin-made clothwork.

FILET LACE (LACIS) AND
BURATO (BURATTO)

FILET LACE

Characteristics

1. Knotted net with regular square meshes and darned (needle-run) patterns.
2. Each mesh has one thread along each side and a knot at each corner. The threads are usually parallel and perpendicular to the length of the lace so that the meshes look square but are sometimes at 45 degrees to the length giving diamond-shaped meshes.
3. The darning threads run in and out of the meshes, mostly parallel to the sides of the meshes.
4. The darning threads are usually similar to the mesh threads but a heavier thread is sometimes used, particularly in German examples to outline designs.

Points to watch

Filet lace is easily distinguished from Burato and from a 19th-century copy made on a net curtain machine by the knots at the corners of the meshes.

History

The making of knotted nets is an old craft, used for centuries in the fishing industry, in agriculture and for household purposes, but its use in household decoration probably began in the 15th or 16th century. The net, called 'lacis' in Italian or 'filet' in French, decorated with embroidery, was then used in much the same way as cutwork embroidery with which it was often combined.

Filet lace was still popular in the early 17th century but later fell from favour except in peasant communities. In the last quarter of the 19th century it was revived both commercially and as a craft hobby. At this time, ladies unwilling to spend laborious hours hand-knotting the ground could buy it ready-made and concentrate on the more pleasing task of decorating it with embroidery.

Throughout its history, filet lace has been used both for small costume items and for substantial household goods, such as coverlets, curtains and tablecloths. The wide display surfaces of these latter fabrics provided one of the few opportunities in lace textiles for pictorial design. Legends from classical antiquity were particularly common sources of inspiration.

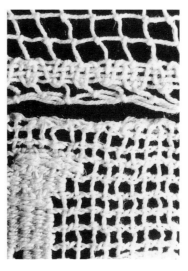

PLATE 60: Detail of Plate 59*a* and *c* showing the knotted ground of filet lace (above) in comparison with the woven burato ground (below).

PLATE 59:
a. Filet lace edging: late 19th C.
    Depth 9 cm (3.6 in)
    Pattern repeat 15 cm (6 in)
The darning thread is of the same weight as the ground thread and is darned in two directions parallel to the sides of the meshes. The simple, repeated floral motif is typically 19th-century in character.

b. Filet lace edging: probably 18th C.
    Depth 7.5 cm (3 in)
    Pattern repeat 14.5 cm (5.7 in)
Heavy darning threads are worked through the ground regardless of the direction of the meshes which are arranged to appear diamond shaped. The design is a derivative of the 17th-century Italianate baroque laces but is poorly drawn and coarse compared with the originals; this suggests a peasant origin, perhaps German from the use of thick darning threads.

c. Burato edging: late 16th–early 17th C.
    Depth 13.5 cm (5.3 in)
    Pattern repeat 24 cm (9.5 in)
The stylized plant forms arranged in alternate orientations are typical of late 16th-century designs, in general, but are not illustrated elsewhere in this book since they are not commonly found in true laces.

BURATO

Characteristics of Burato

1. Square-meshed, open-weave fabric with darned, or needle-run, patterns.
2. Each mesh is bounded by one thread on two sides and by two threads crossed on the other two sides.
3. The darning is similar to that in filet lace.
4. Coloured threads, particularly silk, are found more often than in other lace-like fabrics.

History

Whereas filet lace was made throughout Europe, Burato appears to be a product specifically of Italy. In the 16th and 17th centuries, the woven Burato mesh was decorated with needlework in exactly the same way as filet and often to the same designs. Like filet lace, it went out of fashion in the late 17th century but continued in the peasant tradition, the same designs being repeated time and again in the 18th century so that dating surviving examples is nigh impossible.

Although some Burato was made in the craft revival of the late 19th century it never regained the popularity of filet lace.

LACE KNITTING

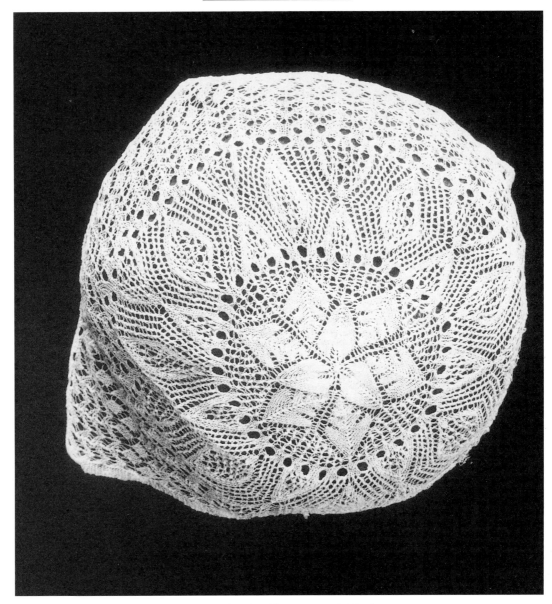

PLATE 61: **Bonnet knitted in white cotton: probably about
1830–50.**
Diameter of circular back 7 cm (3 in)

Characteristics

Knitted textiles consist of interlinked rows of looped
stitches but, unlike needle lace which is worked on a
pattern, knitting is created in the hand from instructions
which the worker must read or memorize. Normally the
stitches are pulled tightly together to form a solid fabric,
with designs created more by the use of colour than of
texture. Lace knitting, on the other hand, relies for its
decorative effect on contrasts between areas of varying
density and texture created by the different ways in which
stitches are cross-linked.

History

Although knitting itself is an old craft, lace knitting seems to
have developed in the second half of the 18th century when
there was a vogue for lighter laces and for the geometric
designs to which this craft is suited. It remained popular in
the 19th century and became a cottage industry in the
Shetland Isles in the second half of the century when the fine
wool from the Shetland sheep was found to be suitable for
shawls and Scottish wedding veils; these, though perhaps six
feet square, could be pulled through a wedding ring.

MACRAMÉ AND TATTING

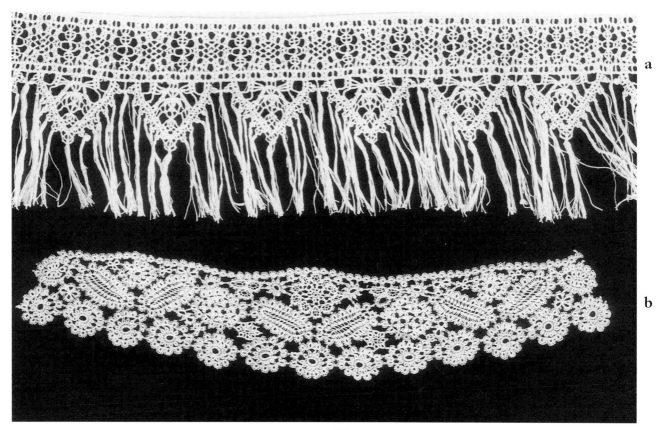

PLATE 62:

a. Macramé edging: late 17th or 18th C.
    Maximum depth of macramé edging excluding fringe 9.5 cm
      (3.7 in)
The macramé is worked separately and sewn on to the linen rather
than being worked in the free warp threads of the linen, as is
sometimes the case.

b. Tatting: late 19th C.
    Length 44 cm (17.5 in)
    Maximum depth 9 cm (3.5 in)

MACRAMÉ

Characteristics

1. A knotted work made with a multitude of threads,
mainly in geometric designs.

In macramé work, a number of threads are first supported
so that they lie parallel to each other and adjacent threads are
then knotted together in various combinations. Short
lengths at the free ends of the threads are often left loose as a
fringe.

History

Macramé was certainly known in the 16th century when the
threads used were often the free warp threads at the end of a
woven fabric. Its use continued throughout the 17th century
and into the 18th century. After a period of decline, it was
revived as a domestic craft in the second half of the 19th
century. Many examples in coarse string survive from this
period while in recent years there has been a vogue for
macramé lampshades and hanging supports for plant pots.

TATTING

Characteristics

1. A knotted lace made with a thread usually carried on,
and worked with the aid of, a tatting shuttle.

2. Designs of knotted rings, often with circular loops of
thread (picots) projecting from the rings; smaller rings are
connected together to form larger circles, ovals and other
geometric shapes.

History

The exact origin of tatting is unclear but it was certainly
known by the mid-19th century and was a common pastime
in the second half of the century. Some tatting was also
carried out professionally.

IRISH CROCHET

PLATE 63:

a. Irish crochet cuff: late 19th–early 20th C.
    Depth at centre 12 cm (4.5 in)
    Width 25 cm (10 in)
The roses formed by concentric rings of overlapping petals are
typical of Irish crochet as is the ground of irregular meshes
formed by crocheted picot bars. Crochet with these features was
still being made and sold in Ireland only a few years ago.

b. Flounce of Irish crochet in cream silk thread: about 1880–1900.
    Maximum depth 12 cm (4.8 in)
    Pattern repeat 15 cm (6 in)
The use of silk thread is supposed to have been introduced by
Messrs. Hayward of Oxford Street, London, one of the many
influential London shops which marketed lace from all parts of
Europe. Although not a close copy, the design is inspired by 17th-
century Venetian needlepoints and includes some padded raised
work.

Characteristics

1. Fabric of linked chain stitches formed with a hooked needle.
2. Pattern motifs are often joined by picoted brides sometimes linked into coarse, irregular meshes.

Technique

Like knitting, crochet is worked in the hand from a set of read or memorized instructions. Simple designs can be worked in long lengths, but more complex designs are divided into motifs which are connected at a later stage.

Points to watch

In Ireland crochet was developed until almost any guipure needlelace could be copied, from the heaviest, most thickly padded to the finest of the Venetian needlepoints. Its looped chain stitch creates a closer imitation of needlework than any other technique and can easily fool the unwary, particularly when the motifs are joined by needle-made bars or decorated with buttonholed rings as is sometimes the case.

PLATE 64: **Detail of Plate 63a** showing the interlinked looped stitches created by the crochet hook, raised flower petals and padded rings, here covered with crochet stitches which create a chain-stitch outline and picoted frills, different from a buttonholed outline.

History

Crochet is an old craft, known in the 17th century and perhaps earlier but its popularity grew only in the mid-19th century. In England and in other parts of Europe it was used mainly to make edgings for household linen in simple repetitive designs.

Only in Ireland did it develop its true potential. Here, in 1845, a school was established in Blackrock, County Cork, as one of the many famine-relief measures of the period. The craft quickly became popular and spread to other parts of Ireland as, unlike the net embroidery crafts (pages 74–80), it required little equipment and could easily be worked at home.

It is not clear how the crochet technique came to be adapted to copying needle-made laces but this must have been influenced by the contemporary growth of the Irish needlepoint industry (pages 58–9). Certainly, among the earliest crochet laces were copies of late 17th-century Venetian flat points in undistinguished designs of small crescents joined by irregular meshes. Before long padded rings were added and the heavier Venetian rose points were copied.

These new, complex designs could not be worked satisfactorily in continuous lengths and were split into small parts which were then joined together. A further innovation was the 'raised rose', a flower formed by concentric circles of raised petals which is found in almost all Irish crochets with floral designs.

Although the new raised crochet was well received in Europe, it was slow and difficult to make compared with household edgings for which there was also a ready market. Many workers therefore turned to these poorer-quality products and, in the 1870s, the Irish crochet industry shared the decline of so many European lace industries.

Fortunately, the revival of interest in lace in the 1880s favoured the heavy guipures which could be copied effectively, and comparatively cheaply, by the crochet technique and by the 1900s even large costume items, such as jackets and shawl collars, were being made. The Irish industry recovered some of its prosperity and has continued, if on a much reduced scale, to the present day.

Although Ireland was pre-eminent in the technique, raised crochet was copied widely in Europe, both as a craft hobby and on a commercial scale. Only a few years ago I came across a town in Italy where 'punto d'Irlande' was still being made. It was a fascinating derivative: here was a craft inspired by 17th-century Venetian needlepoints, overlaid by Irish features and now again used in imitations of the earlier laces but with a decidedly 20th-century, Italianate flavour.

EMBROIDERED MACHINE NETS

a   b

TAMBOURED NET

Characteristics

1. Chain-stitch embroidery carried out with a hooked needle on machine-made net.
2. Lines of linked chain loops are visible on the right side of the fabric and lines of close, straight stitches on the wrong side.
3. Areas of fancy filling stitches, often darned in, are common (pages 76–7).
4. A hand- or machine-made picot edging is often sewn around the edge of an article.

Points to watch

Tamboured net can be almost impossible to distinguish from net embroidered by machine; even a machine's supposed regularity of stitch and performance does not always help. Some of the earliest hand sewing machines used a single thread to create a chain stitch identical to that made with a tambour hook and, when they came into widespread use in Europe in the 1860s, they were sometimes used to decorate net. For this purpose, a pattern was drawn on the net and the machine's needle guided along its lines by eye. Needless to say, similar deviations from the true pattern occurred as in tambour work in which a pattern is followed in the same way.

What, then, of regularity of stitch? The earliest machines did not always create regular stitches because of difficulties with their feed mechanisms and a good tambour worker would have prided herself on her ability to work into every mesh, or alternate mesh, of a net.

In the late 19th century multi-needle industrial machines were developed and used to embroider very repetitive designs in both chain and darning stitches. Here the regularity of the work is a true and obvious indication of origin.

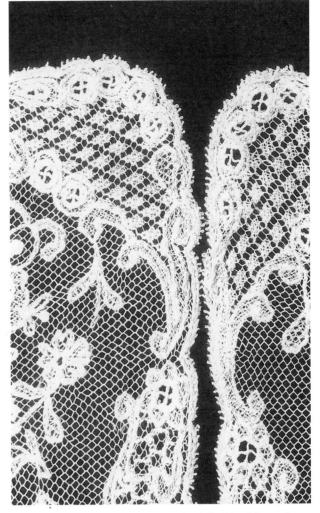

PLATE 66: Detail of Plate 65 showing the right side of the work to the left and the wrong side of the work to the right. The net always makes the two sides difficult to distinguish but the chain stitches are visible on the surface on the right side while lines of straight stitches lie over the surface on the wrong side.

PLATE 65:

a. (*outer*). Handkerchief with edging of machine-made net decorated with tambour work and darned fillings; possibly Limerick: about 1840–60.
   Full width (not shown) 47 cm (18.5 in)
   Depth of net edging 7 cm (2.5 in)

b. (*inner*). Handkerchief with edging of machine-made net decorated with chain-stitch embroidery; probably tamboured: 1870–90.
   Full width (not shown) 34 cm (13.5 in)
   Depth of net edging 9.5 cm (3.7 in)

History (see also page 77)

Tambour work was introduced into Europe from the near East in the early 18th century and derives its name from the tambour (drum)-like frame which supported and stretched the fabric to be embroidered during working. The embroidery itself is carried out with a hooked needle, like a crochet hook but sharper because of its initial use to embroider woven fabrics which needed to be pierced.

In the late 18th century, tamboured whitework on fine lawns and muslins was particularly popular and this no doubt contributed to the transfer of the technique on to machine nets as they became available. Certainly, by the 1810s, the tamboured net industry was well established alongside that of darning on net and from that time their histories are interlinked.

In the early years of their manufacture, the novelty of embroidered nets made them fashionable in even the highest circles of society and they were widely used for bonnet veils, stoles and many other dress accessories. To make the larger items the net was stretched on long frames, sometimes big enough for several workers to sit at together. Work on this scale was, of necessity, carried out in workshops as the frames could not be accommodated in small cottages.

By the middle of the century the novelty had worn off but embroidered nets were still in demand. Together with the patterned machine laces now available, they provided a cheap alternative to 'real lace' for many people who wished to be fashionable but could not afford the completely hand-made article. Lace was no longer the exclusive prerogative of a wealthy and aristocratic minority and this was its downfall.

For a brief period in the 1870s and 1880s, lace was out of fashion. By the 1890s, when it had regained favour, many of the hand-lace industries had declined to such an extent that they were unable to recover. In an age of machine lace, tamboured and needle-run nets had the advantage of being hand-embroidered and this gave them a cachet which maintained their popularity up till the First World War.

NEEDLE-RUN OR DARNED NET

Characteristics

1. Hand embroidery on machine-made net.
2. Pattern threads run, or darned, in and out of the meshes of the net.
3. Areas of fancy filling stitches are common; in some of these the embroidery threads are used to pull larger holes in the net.
4. A hand- or machine-made picot edging is often sewn around the edge of an article.
5. Often combined with tambour work (see pages 74–76).

Points to watch

Embroidery darned on a machine net can look deceptively like a true bobbin lace, especially when worked in simple designs with little clothwork and few filling stitches, or in floss silk in imitation of blonde laces. Look for the way the design threads run in and out of the net in an embroidered example but are caught between other threads in a bobbin lace. Also, check whether a picot edging is made integrally or added on.

Needlerun threads were used to outline designs in the early patterned machine laces to imitate the gimp threads of bobbin laces (see pages 182 and 183) and picot edgings were also added to these.

History (see also tamboured net)

Hand-knotted nets had long been decorated with needle-run embroidery (see filet lace, pages 68–69) when machine-made nets were introduced in the second half of the 18th century and provided a new foundation for this type of work.

The earliest of these nets easily unravelled and little has survived but, by the 1790s, more stable nets were being made on the stocking frame (point net) and on the warp machine (warp net). Both the point and warp nets had a looped construction and were readily distinguishable from hand-made bobbin nets but, in 1809, John Heathcoat patented a machine which manufactured a net substantially identical to the East Midlands point (or Lille) bobbin net. This was to become the most popular ground for both needlework and appliqué laces (see Honiton and Brussels laces) until the advent of a much lighter net with a diamond-shaped mesh in the 1830s.

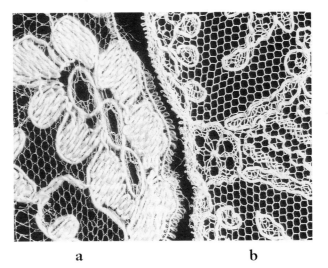

a   b

PLATE 68:

a. Detail of a collar of needle-run net. The coarse thread used in this example can clearly be seen running in and out of the meshes of the net.

b. Detail of an edging of machine-made silk net copying a kat stitch ground darned with a floss silk in imitation of bobbin-made blonde laces. Compare the wavy appearance of the floss silk as it runs in and out of the net with the smooth surface of the blonde lace in Plate 149.

Much of the early development of the net- and lace-making machinery occurred in Nottingham and this became the main centre of the needle-run and tamboured-net industries in England. Coggeshall in Essex was also a noted centre in the first half of the 19th century while London produced goods of particularly high quality.

The famous Limerick industry in County Cork, Ireland, was established in 1829 by an Englishman, Charles Walker. It produced nets embroidered both by needle-running and tambouring, often in combination: the tambouring usually formed the outlines of the designs and the needle-running the fancy fillings. This industry thrived until the 1850s when a lack of new designs and a drop in the standard of workmanship caused its decline but it was revived in the 1880s and survived well into this century.

Embroidery on net was not confined to the British Isles. France and Belgium, in particular, both had flourishing industries making not only the shawls, flounces, collars and trimmings required for fashionable dress but also household goods, such as tamboured net curtains. The advantage given by good designers working for the lace industry as a whole enabled the French and Belgian industries to continue even through the slump of the 1870s. As we have seen, this was in part caused by the embroidered net itself.

PLATE 67: Stole of needle-run machine net: 1825–40.

    Width 41 cm (16 in)

    Length 218 cm (86 in)

    Length of patterned end 43 cm (17 in)

The curved sprig motifs used here are typical of designs of the late 1820s and 1830s. Unusually, the three sprigs are different but are repeated at the opposite end of the stole. Note the variety of filling stitches in the sprigs and in the border which surrounds the entire stole. The picot edging is bobbin-made.

CARRICKMACROSS

Characteristics

1. Cutwork embroidery, in some cases applied to machine-made net.
2. Pattern areas of woven fabric.
3. Pattern outlined with a thick thread couched on to the surface.
4. Article often outlined by picots formed by loops of the outlining thread.
5. Grounds:
   a. Brides, or bars, usually covered with closely-spaced buttonhole stitches and often decorated with picots.
   b. Machine-made net.
6. Fillings:
   a. In guipure forms, needlepoint lace fillings are sometimes found.
   b. Forms with a net ground often include needle-run fillings (see pages 76–77) and areas of guipure work.

Technique

In Carrickmacross appliqué work, a layer of net and an upper layer of muslin or other fine, woven material are tacked on to a pattern and a thick outlining thread is couched on to lines within and around the design: the couching stitches pass through both the woven fabric and the net to sew them together. Unwanted muslin is then cut away, both around the outline and in spaces to be decorated with filling stitches; in some areas both the muslin and the net may be cut away to form a guipure. A pair of special scissors with a knob on one point is used for the task to prevent any accidental cutting of the fabrics.

The filling stitches are usually effected by the needle-running technique on remaining areas of net but parts where both net and muslin have been cut away may be filled with needlepoint stitches. Where wide areas of net and muslin are cut away, the spaces are crossed by needleworked brides which are normally worked before the cutting stage to ensure that the work remains flat when lifted from the pattern.

In the guipure form of Carrickmacross lace, the net is omitted entirely. The outlining thread is couched on to the muslin and the brides which are to connect the various parts of the design are worked before the unwanted muslin is cut away.

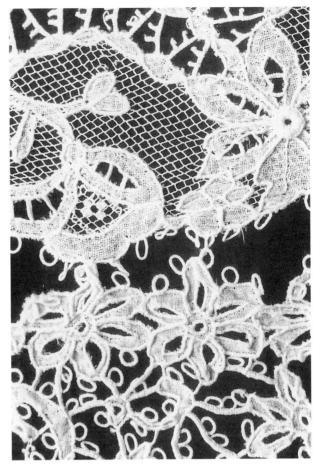

PLATE 69:

a. Detail of Plate 70. The machine-net foundation can be seen through the sheer muslin used for the pattern.

b. Detail of a Carrickmacross guipure edging. The woven muslin and couched outlining thread of Carrickmacross work can be seen more clearly without the foundation net.

Points to watch

The fabric areas of cutwork embroideries are easily distinguishable from bobbin clothwork since the fabric threads are all evenly spaced and run in the same two mutually-perpendicular directions over the entire area of the work, regardless of the design. In bobbin clothwork, the spacing and directions of the threads vary even in straight laces.

The technique of cutwork embroidery on net with a couched thread outline was introduced into Ireland from Italy and continued in use on the continent although a chain-stitched outline worked with a tambour hook or a machine is more usually associated with continental work (see Plate 71).

PLATE 70:
a. Collar of Carrickmacross work: about 1890–1900
   Maximum width 56 cm (22 in)
   Full length 22 cm (8.5 in)
The large size and lobed shape of this collar date it to about the 1890s. It is worked as a muslin appliqué on net with both the net and muslin cut away to form the guipure areas. The fancy fillings are of needle-run embroidery.

History

In the 1820s, Mrs Porter of Donaghmoyne, who is said to have acquired a novel piece of applied muslin on machine-made net on her travels in Italy, taught the technique to local women in an attempt to provide a form of gainful employment in a period of depression. The scheme was dependent on private orders and was of limited success but, with the potato famines of the 1840s, a more businesslike approach was taken with the setting up of lace schools on the Bath and Shirley Estates at Carrickmacross.

Here the appliqué work, subsequently to be known as 'Carrickmacross' lace, was taught and the guipure form developed. The products of this work had an initial period of success which was followed by a decline, as in the Limerick industry, due to a fall in the standards of workmanship and design. Revivals in the 1880s and, in particular, in the 1890s when great care was taken over design, led to the production of large quantities of fine quality goods which found ready markets abroad and also resulted in the survival of the industry in Ireland to the present day.

PLATE 71: **Detail of continental appliqué work in which the muslin is applied to a machine-made net by means of a chain stitch.**

BOBBIN LACES

TORCHON

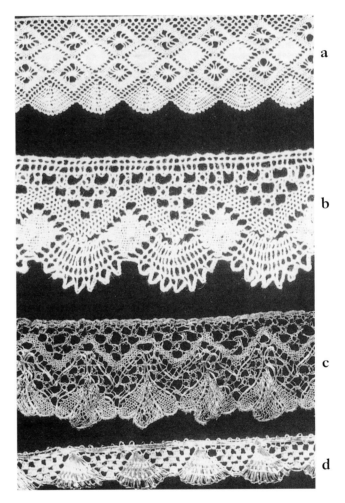

Characteristics
1. Straight bobbin lace in a variety of threads.
2. Cloth stitch and half stitch pattern areas.
3. Largely geometric designs.
4. Usually made with uniform threads, with no raised work, but a gimp thread or raised tallies (see Plate 72b) are sometimes incorporated.
5. Ground: large-scale meshes. The torchon ground, unusually for bobbin laces, is worked at 45 degrees to the edge and has roughly square meshes with two threads crossing on each side.

History
Laces with the characteristic geometric designs of torchon laces have been known since at least the 17th century but in the mid-19th century they became particularly popular and acquired the name 'torchon'. Being the simplest of the bobbin laces, they could be made quickly and cheaply and became the mainstay of many lacemaking areas in Europe as the competition from machine laces forced workers to turn away from the more difficult laces which were rapidly becoming uneconomic.

PLATE 72: Group of torchon edgings.
a. In cotton thread; late 19th–20th C.
     Maximum depth 5.5 cm (2.2 in)
The design consists of cloth stitch diamonds, half stitch diamonds filled with 'spiders', fans along the scalloped edge and triangles of torchon ground along the footside.

b. In cream worsted wool.
     Maximum depth 10 cm (4 in)
Laces in worsted wool were known as 'yak' laces and were worked in torchon and other simple designs. Black yak laces were often used on mourning dress, particularly on outer garments.

c. In gold thread; 18th or 19th C.
     Maximum depth 6.5 cm (2.5 in)
The gold thread for this type of lace was usually made by

wrapping a narrow strip of gold foil around a fibre core, commonly of silk. The stiffness of the resulting thread meant that it was unsuitable for complicated designs.

At times gold and silver thread laces were worn in such quantities that strict laws (sumptuary laws) were promulgated to restrict the quantity and quality worn by different ranks. The restrictions in the 16th and 17th centuries probably played a part in the development of more elaborate lace designs which could be achieved in the supple linen and silk threads.

d. In silver thread; 19th or 20th C.
     Maximum depth 3 cm (1.2 in)
This lace includes thread made like the gold thread of example (c) above, but also narrow strips of silver foil.

EARLY BOBBIN LACES IN GEOMETRIC AND SIMPLE TRAIL DESIGNS AND LATER COPIES

Characteristics

1. Straight or semi-straight bobbin lace.
2. Made with uniform threads.
3. Simple patterns formed by narrow, trailing lines of clothwork connected by plaited and twisted bars and wheatears.
4. Little use of raised work or of fancy filling stitches other than wheatears.
5. Found as straight-edged insertions and pointed and scalloped edgings with a symmetrical design repeated in each point or scallop.
6. A footing is often worked integrally with the lace.

Points to watch

It is difficult to distinguish early Flemish examples from Italian ones but, as with needlepoints, the Italian work is often tighter: this can make the clothwork pucker. Also, Italian laces include pointed wheatears more often than Flemish laces.

Early laces are often semi-straight, with sewings joining touching parts: 19th- and 20th-century examples are more usually straight laces.

PLATE 73:

a. Edging: probably late 16th C: Flemish?
   Depth 3.2 cm (1.3 in)
The lower geometric border is sewn to a later 17th century insertion.

b. (upper left). Insertion: 17th C or 18th C peasant lace in the late 16th C style.
   Depth 3 cm (1.1 in)

c. (lower left). Insertion: probably late 16th C, in a style seen in pattern books from about 1560 onwards: probably Italian.
   Depth 3 cm (1.1 in)

d. (right). Insertion: probably early 17th C in a style of about 1610–40: Northern Italian.
   Depth 5.5 cm (2.2 in)
The design of rosettes in rectangular compartments is copied from reticella designs (pages 16–21). The pointed wheatears are particularly associated with Genoese work.

e. (centre). Edging: 17th C, in the pointed style of the last quarter of the 16th C: North Italian.
   Maximum depth 6 cm (2.3 in)

f. Edging: 17th C or later, in the style of the early 17th C: probably Italian.
   Maximum depth 3.5 cm (1.3 in)

g. Edging: about 1610–30: Italian or Flemish.
   Maximum depth 6 cm (2.3 in)
The thread and tightness of working of these pieces show them all to be of early date but b, d, e, and f are in coarser threads than would have been used on fashionable dress; they could have been made for household or church linen or for peasant dress at a later date than suggested by their designs. (See also Plate 7c and Plate 74c.)

History

Bobbin laces appear to have developed in the 16th century, probably from plaited and woven braids, and at first had very simple, basically geometric designs. Many of these were made in silk or metal thread and were applied as surface decoration to the rich fabrics of the period. Others, in linen thread, were used as insertions in domestic linen but it may not have been until about the 1570s that bobbin laces were used as decorative edgings. Many of the portraits after this time, however, show ruffs bordered by spiky laces formed by very narrow lines, different from those of contemporary needlepoints.

It is uncertain whether Northern Italy or Flanders first produced these bobbin laces; as with the needle laces, early references occur in the records of both regions. In Italy the main centres were Genoa and Milan but Venice also made bobbin lace while many of the Flemish towns which later became famous for specific types of lace had industries in this early period.

In the early 17th century the geometric style was still popular. If anything, designs for insertion laces became more rigidly organized into rectangular compartments filled with repeated, rosette-like motifs in imitation of the reticella needlepoints. These are perhaps most effective in the tightly worked Italian laces, particularly those with a proliferation of wheatears (Plate 73d) which may be Genoese.

At the same time, freer designs were developing. This was a natural trend in the bobbin laces which, unlike the reticella needlepoints, did not have the constraint of a fabric foundation. The first signs are seen in the 16th-century edgings where the narrow tapes or plaits twist to and fro, working down one edge of a point and up the other.

As the early pointed edgings gradually gave way in the 17th century to tiny, rounded scallops or pointed arches, floral motifs became more common but designs formed by tapes which snaked from one scallop to the next, forming a symmetrical, geometric pattern in each scallop, continued into the 1640s. This was particularly true of Northern laces but, as the scallops became shallower, the designs, which had been very open in the 1620s and 1630s, became more crowded and the spaces between the tapes became filled with an early form of mesh ground.

By the mid-17th century, simple, geometric designs were no longer fashionable but they persisted in coarser, household laces or in peasant communities, in some regions even into the 19th century. Indeed, it was Genoa that supplied the lace makers who started the Maltese industry in the 1830s (pages 170–2). The success of this industry was due, in part, to a renewed interest in guipure laces but the products of the 1840s and 1850s were generally more complex than the laces seen in Plate 73. In the 1860s laces closely resembling the early laces were produced at Mirecourt, the centre of the French lace industry of Lorraine. These products, known as 'Cluny laces', were copied from antique laces in the Cluny Museum in Paris, it is said.

The mid-19th century was a period of massive expansion in the lace trade but also a time when the hand-lace industry was suffering greatly from competition with cheaper machine laces. Many of the makers of poorer-quality laces turned to easier, more quickly made products to scrape a living and Cluny laces and their derivatives became the staple product of many lace-making areas of Europe. The laces made in the different areas are often indistinguishable from each other but they were cheap products, largely made for the home market, and are likely to have been made where they are now found. They were worked in black and white cotton, cream and black silk and other threads.

The Cluny and related guipures are usually readily distinguishable from their 16th- and 17th-century counterparts by their thread and their workmanship, but this is not always true. The interest in antique laces in the 1850s and again in the 1880s and 1890s led to some close copies of the old designs being made in fine linen thread. When trying to date lace one must always be on one's guard.

FIGURE 12: Woman's falling collar and whisk; about 1625–45. The change in men's dress in the 1620s (see Figure 3) was matched by a similar change in women's dress. The deep neckline of the bodice became edged with a broad, scalloped band of lace, and a matching collar fell over the shoulders but the neckline was often filled in, at least during the day, with a chemise or undergarment, or was covered by a whisk. This was a square or shaped piece of fine linen, edged with lace and folded roughly into a triangle. It was worn around the neck and often masked the collar, except for the horizontal fall at the front.

PLATE 74:
a. Edging: early 20th C in the style of the 1620s.
   Depth 8.5 cm (3.3 in)
The design of this example is copied exactly from a 1620s pattern; only the thread betrays its 20th-century origin. This has turned brown, which is typical of thread used by workers organized by the Aemelia Ars Society in Bologna in the early 20th century.

b. Collar: 1850–70: probably English, East Midlands.
   Maximum width 31 cm (12.2 in)
   Depth of lace scallops 5.5 cm (2.2 in)
The close similarity of the lace design to that of the edging in Plate 73g will be apparent, but this collar could have been made only in the 19th century, most probably in the middle years when fashion required neat, round collars, which fitted closely round the high necks of day dresses.

c. Insertion and edging joined.
Insertion: early 17th C in an alternating geometric design: Italian, possibly Genoese.
   Depth 2.2 cm (0.8 in)
Edging: late 19th C in the style of about 1630–50.
   Maximum depth 5.5 cm (2.1 in)
This combination demonstrates a further trap for the unwary: the edging and insertion could, stylistically, be of the same date. Only the difference in feel and quality of the threads points to their differing ages, and this can be judged only by experience.

d. Edging: late 19th C.
   Depth 8 cm (3.2 in)
This shows the type of design most usually referred to as 'Cluny' because of the inclusion of a divided trail of clothwork (the two clothwork tapes separated by a row of holes). This example is probably English East Midlands work.

a

b

c

d

MILANESE AND NORTH ITALIAN

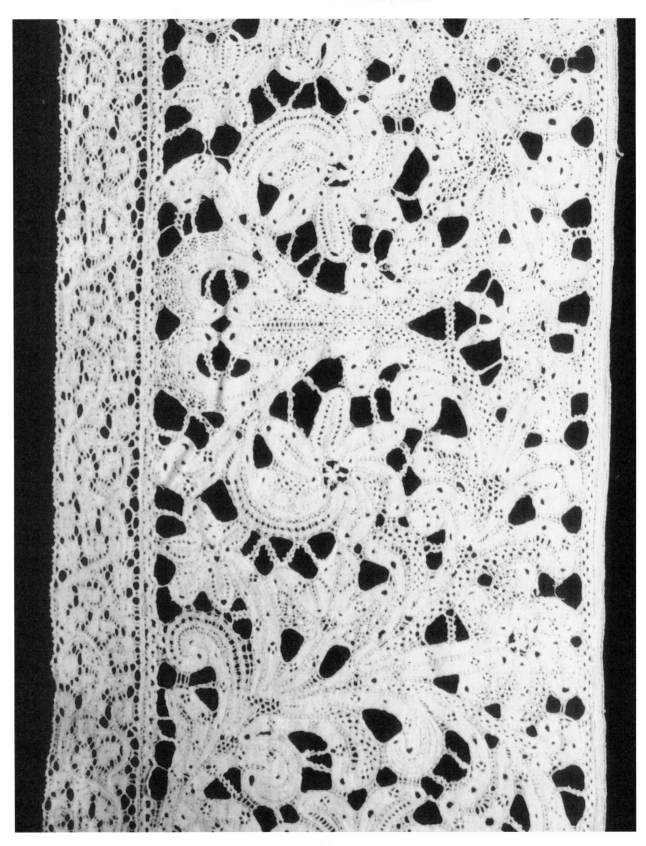

Characteristics

1. Semi-straight or part bobbin lace.
2. Flat lace with uniform threads.
3. Pattern of scrolling clothwork often formed by a continuous tape.
4. Fillings formed by arrays of holes in the clothwork and areas of fancy stitches in spaces in the designs.
5. Right and wrong sides differ: the wrong side often has occasional groups of threads passing loosely across it from one area of working to another.
6. Grounds:

    a. Bobbin-made bars often arranged in pairs and decorated with picots (Plate 76). In bolder forms the pattern motifs touch and only a few bars are needed.

    b. Round or diamond mesh ground (Plate 77). The round mesh has four threads plaited or crossed on six sides, enclosing an almost round hole. Clear pinholes are often visible at four corners. When very tightly worked, it can appear diamond shaped.

Points to watch

See Flemish bobbin laces (page 95).

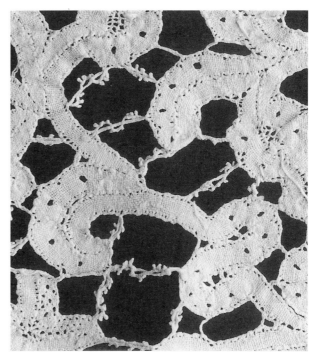

PLATE 76: Detail showing the Italian double-bar ground. The threads are taken across a space from one edge to another and then back before they are worked along the edge to the next point where a bar is needed. They are sometimes carried over the back of the lace but less frequently, and over shorter distances, than in Flemish work.

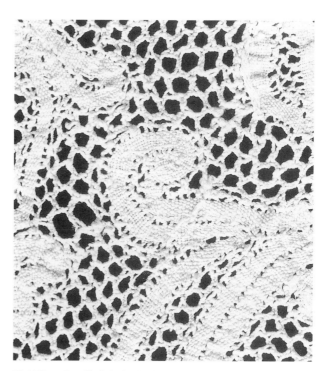

PLATE 75: Milanese flounce with a later Flemish bobbin lace edging: flounce about 1660–80; edging about 1690–1700 (see comment on Plate 121).

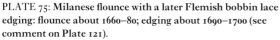

    Depth of flounce 22 cm (8.5 in)
    Pattern repeat 74 cm (29 in)
    Length shown 36 cm (14 in)
    Depth of edging 4.5 cm (1.6 in)

The flounce is made up from separate panels each a single pattern repeat long with a central axis of symmetry: a secondary axis is created at the join. Despite its apparent complexity, the design is formed essentially by a single scrolling tape joined by sewings along touching edges. The contrasting effects are given by variations in the width of the tape itself and in the arrays of holes and filling stitches within it. As is typical of Italian work, the leaves and flowers are formed by the tape branching from a stem and doubling back to form the stem again.

PLATE 77: Detail of the back of the lace in Plate 79c showing the Italian round mesh ground. The ground threads are linked by sewings into the edge of the previously made pattern and occasionally carried loosely over the back.

PLATE 78: Milanese edging: about 1640–50.

Depth 8 cm (3.2 in)

Pattern repeat 8.5 cm (3.4 in)
This piece shows the transition from the simpler, symmetrical plant designs of the early 17th century to the later baroque designs. The slightly wavy headside has replaced the scalloped edge of earlier laces.

Note the slight variation in the width of the clothwork forming the leaves and the minor use of filling stitches and raised work on the surface.

From the collection of Mrs Valerie Cliffe

FIGURE 13: Man's bib-fronted (rabat) collar; about 1660–80.
By the mid-17th century men's hair styles were so long that they concealed any lace at the back of the collar and so interest was focused at the front. The two rectangular panels of the bib-fronted collar displayed the baroque patterns of Italian laces admirably; the panels are joined by a very narrow band which passes round the back of the neck and is tied at the front.

PLATE 79 (OPPOSITE):

a. Milanese edging: about 1650–75.

Depth 8.5 cm (3.4 in)

Pattern repeat 78 cm (31 in)

Length shown 54 cm (21 in)
The bold design with its scrolling motifs and, in particular, the orchid-like flower towards the upper right is typical of the Italian baroque style. Although apparently continuous, the design is worked in short pieces joined together by sewings.

Many of the scrolls are formed by single tapes worked into a centre rather than by double tapes as in the example below. The few connecting brides are pairs of twisted threads.

b. North Italian edging: probably Milanese: 1660–90.

Depth 11 cm (4.5 in)

Pattern repeat 66 cm (26 in)
The pattern repeats about two alternating, symmetrical designs but the curving lines are typically baroque. It is made as a semi-straight lace. To follow the twists and turns of the tape through the design is like following a maze: the tape also forms the heading.

Note the rows of tallies worked over the surface around the flower centres.

c. Edging: probably North Italian: about 1680–1700.

Depth 11 cm (4.2 in)

Pattern repeat 21 cm (8.5 in)
This example, like the central edging, is based on narrow, flowing lines but the scale of the flowers is smaller and there is more space between them so that a ground is essential. It is these factors which suggest a later date for this piece.

The North Italian origin is suggested by the tightness of working, particularly of the mesh ground; the division of the work into small parts and use of single rather than double-tape stems suggest a Flemish origin which is also possible.

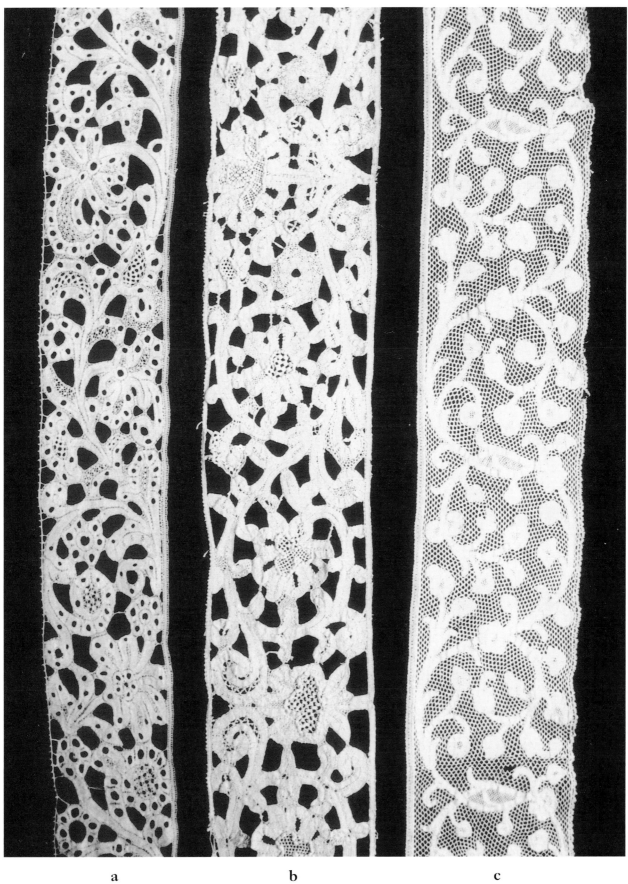

a   b   c

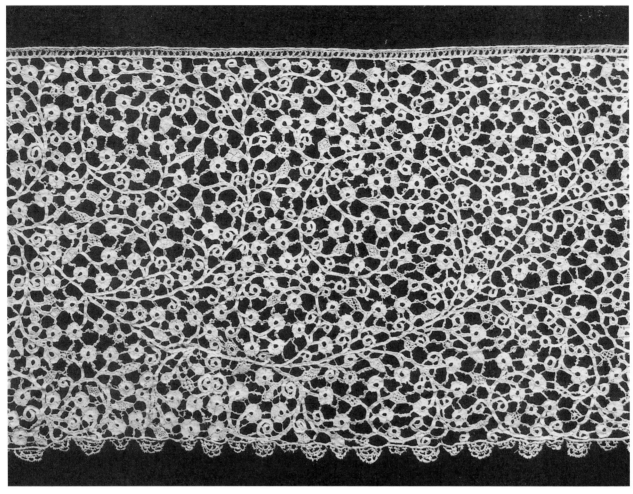

PLATE 80: **Flounce: possibly Venetian bobbin lace: about 1680–1700.**

 Depth 20 cm (8 in)
 Pattern repeat 37 cm (14 in)
 Length shown 33 cm (13 in)

It is known that some bobbin lace was made in Venice and the very close similarity between the design of this type of guipure and the contemporary Venetian needlepoints suggest its Venetian origin.

History

We have already seen how designs changed gradually from the geometric to the baroque style in the 17th-century Venetian needlepoints and this trend occurred simultaneously in the North Italian bobbin laces. As early as the late 16th century, floral motifs had been introduced into the symmetrical designs of pointed and scalloped edgings and by the early 17th century these had developed into more flowing designs of curving, trailing stems bearing small leaves and flowerheads. These could easily be created by the bobbin technique as the narrow tapes required only a small number of bobbins and the motifs could be worked by the semi-straight or part techniques (Plate 78).

As technical abilities improved and the more expensive needlepoint laces were elaborated, so were the bobbin laces; the clothwork pattern areas expanded and holes and filling stitches which had played a minor role in earlier laces assumed greater importance. By the 1650s the baroque style was fully fledged and is seen more clearly in the Milanese bobbin laces than in the Venetian needlepoints where the heavy raised work and later rearrangement of motifs frequently conceal the original design.

As in the needlepoints, the bolder designs of the 1650s to 1670s required few connecting bars and, in Milanese laces, the clear spaces between the smoothly rounded outlines of the motifs were often complemented by large apertures in the clothwork (Plate 79a). In more elaborate forms, the scrolling tapes were patterned by a seemingly endless succession of diverse stitches (Plate 75).

Towards the end of the century, as the scale of the motifs decreased, the variety of filling stitches was reduced and the tapework narrowed to an almost uniform width in all but the more exceptional cases. The number of connecting bars increased but these do not appear to have developed into a net ground; instead, the net ground appears to have developed slightly later but alongside the bar ground. At first the meshes were irregular both in shape and direction

but by the 1670s a more organized round or diamond mesh ground had developed. Alternative nets, such as the kat stitch ground (page 181), were also used occasionally.

By 1700 the Italian baroque style was out of favour in fashionable dress but lace continued to be made in the lighter, open designs of the late 17th century (Plate 79c) through much of the 18th century. At the same time, designs influenced by the new French classical style were seen (Plate 81). In these, narrow tapes meander almost continuously through the lace, defining areas of indeterminate shape filled with fancy stitches, and organized in repeated symmetrical arrangements about vertical axes.

Much of this 18th-century bobbin lace was made in wide flounces for church use whereas narrower, coarser edgings were made and used in the peasant communities. This manufacture spread out from Milan, where the finest of the 17th-century lace was made, north to the Alps and into the southern parts of Austria. Derivatives were also made in Germany and eastern Europe.

In the 19th century the peasant traditions continued in Italy to a limited extent, with a revival at the end of the century, but the 19th-century laces most easily confused with their early predecessors were mainly made in Belgium and are considered in the next chapter.

PLATE 81: Flounce: probably North Italian: about 1700–40, but possibly Flemish.

   Depth 28 cm (11 in)
   Pattern repeat 23 cm (9 in)
   Length shown 40 cm (16 in)

A comparison of this flounce with the Flemish flounce in the 'candelabra' style (Plate 90a) will show the influence of French designs. The differences are that here the branching motifs are created, and joined, by a bobbin-made tape which meanders almost continuously through the design; and many of the budlike flowers are created by loops in the tape.

The scalloped headside is a typical feature of point de France; Italian baroque laces normally have a straight edge. The motifs in the scallops are worked separately, as are the major panels which are joined by the ground and the fillings along secondary axes of symmetry in the design.

FLEMISH LACES IN THE ITALIAN BAROQUE AND FRENCH STYLES

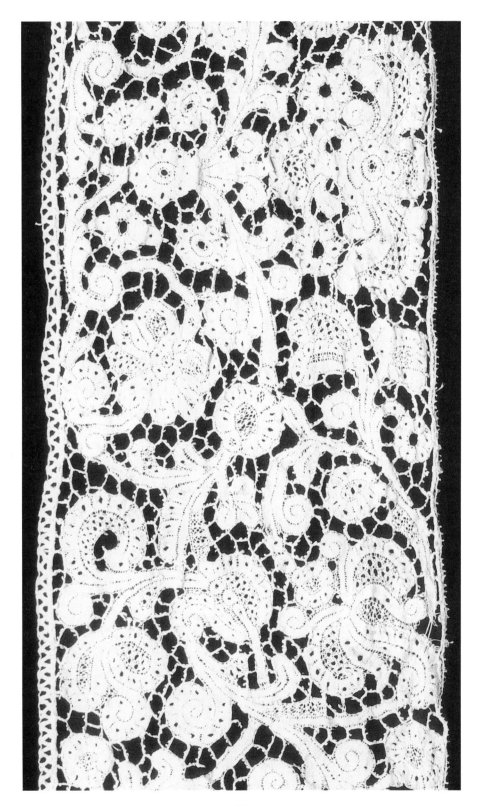

Characteristics

1. Usually a part lace but occasionally semi-straight.

2. Made with uniform threads.

3. Mainly flat but with some Brussels-type raised work after about 1700.

4. Clothwork pattern areas with some half stitch after about 1700.

5. Right and wrong sides differ: the wrong side has groups of threads passing loosely across it from one area of working to another; the right side may have raised outlines in later examples.

6. Grounds:

    a. Bobbin-made bars, often decorated with picots (Plate 83).

    b. Round mesh ground (Plate 84). Hexagonal mesh with four threads plaited or crossed on all six sides, enclosing an almost round hole with pinholes usually visible at each corner. A very open variation, similar to kat stitch (see page 181) is often found, particularly in 18th-century examples.

Note. The division between the laces described here and those described on pages 131–5 is somewhat arbitrary because of the mixture of techniques and styles current in 17th century Flemish laces. Some separation is useful, however, and the Flemish-style laces lead conveniently on to the straight laces considered in the later chapters.

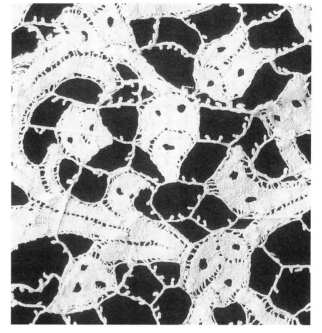

PLATE 83: Detail of the reverse of the lace in Plate 85*b* showing the typical Flemish bar ground: the bars are worked in continuous lengths after the pattern has been completed and are joined by sewings into the edges of the motifs. They are decorated with picots where they cross the spaces between motifs and are worked along the edges or carried across the backs of the motifs from one point where they are needed to the next.

Note the cut ends of thread in the clothwork areas where threads have been removed during working as the clothwork is narrowed.

PLATE 82: **Flounce of Flemish bobbin lace: about 1660–80.**
  Depth 18 cm (7 in)
  Length shown 34 cm (13.5 in)
  Pattern repeat 83 cm (33 in)
This flounce displays a typically Flemish treatment of the Italian baroque style yet individual features such as the part-lace technique, the leaf scrolls and the symmetry of the design about the motif on the right can all be found in Italian laces.

    Many of the brides in this piece are not original and the rest of the flounce (not shown) is in poor condition.

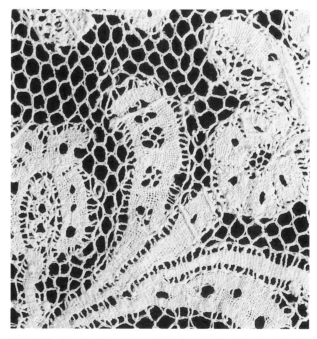

PLATE 84: Detail of the reverse of the lace in Plate 85*a* showing the loose working of the Flemish 'round' mesh ground. Like the bar ground, the threads of the mesh ground are joined by sewings to the threads outlining the design and are occasionally carried loosely over the backs of the motifs from one area of working to the next.

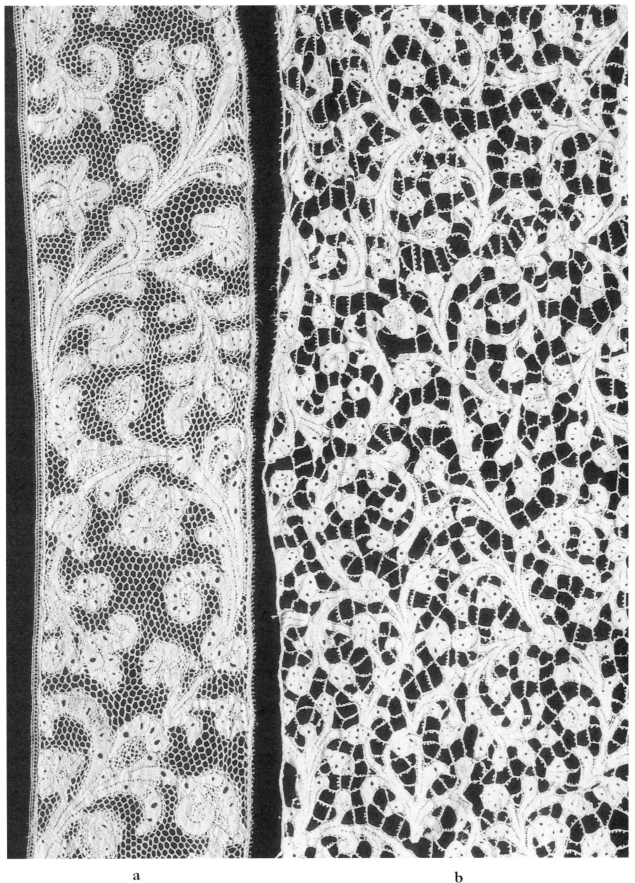

a

b

Points to watch

Flemish bobbin laces in Italianate baroque designs are confusingly similar to their Italian counterparts but the following indications can help to distinguish them:

(*a*) Italian laces tend to be more tightly worked than Flemish ones; this may be noticeable in densely packed clothwork, strong bars and tightly plaited meshes in which the pinholes at two corners disappear.

(*b*) Italian bars are often in pairs whereas Flemish bars are more usually single.

(*c*) Flemish designs tend to include more intersecting stems: Italian designs have a more continuous flow and backward-curving motifs rarely cross other motifs.

(*d*) Flemish designs tend to be broken into smaller parts for working.

(*e*) Flemish scrolls are often formed by a single stem spiralling into a centre, whereas Italian scrolls more often have a double stem spiralling into and out from the centre.

(*f*) Flemish laces are often in a finer thread and tend to be softer and more supple than Italian laces.

It must be remembered that these are tendencies, not hard rules; there are exceptions to all of them.

PLATE 85:
a. Flemish edging: about 1670–90.
   Depth 9.5 cm (3.7 in)
   Pattern repeat 73 cm (29 in)
   Length shown 35.5 cm (14 in)
Although the design flows continuously, the lace is made in relatively small parts.

b. Part of a Flemish flounce (altered): about 1690–1700.
   Depth shown 15 cm (6 in)
This example is very typical of Flemish lace in the Italian style of the late 17th century; the thread is finer, the clothwork broader than in Italian lace; the rounded flower buds divided into lobes, each with a central hole, are characteristic and also found in contemporary Flemish laces in the French style (Plate 90a).

History of Flemish laces in the Italian baroque style

The term Flemish bobbin laces is used very generally to identify all those 16th- and 17th-century laces made in the Low Countries, particularly in Flanders, before the various lace-making towns such as Brussels, Mechlin and Valenciennes had developed their own peculiar characteristics. It therefore includes the early geometric laces already described, as well as laces in the Italian baroque manner and laces in floral designs peculiar to Northern Europe (see pages 132–5). It also includes late 17th-century laces in the French manner, which are considered separately.

In the earlier years, while techniques were developing, there was no clear distinction between straight, part and semi-straight laces but in the mid-17th century their paths diverged. Although the baroque style influenced the straight laces, it is seen in perhaps its most accomplished form in the part laces. Here the division of the work into separate motifs enabled each to be patterned with intricate detail while the essential rhythm and movement of the baroque could be achieved by their subsequent combination into large, flowing designs.

Naturally the Flemish baroque laces followed the same design trends as their Italian counterparts and the origins of many surviving examples, especially those of poorer quality, are unclear. Some indications of differences are given under Points to Watch but qualities such as the tightness of working can be judged only by experience.

Perhaps one innovation of the Flemish industry was the net ground. This had started to develop before 1650 and was formed in various ways before it settled into the most common form, known as the round ground. The Italian ground is very similar; did it develop independently? As yet there is no clear answer.

By 1700 the baroque designs had dwindled into patterns of branching, curving stems carrying tiny bud-like flowers and in Flanders a different influence was being felt: that of France. The new French designs started a fresh fashion to which we shall return later. In the meantime, designs similar to that shown in Plate 79c continued to be made into the 18th century and were joined by scrolling tape designs, such as that in Plate 86, which combined the Italian and the new French styles.

It was not until the late 19th century that interest in the Italian baroque style returned. The major demand at this time was for heavy Venetian needlepoints but bobbin laces in imitation of the Milanese were also made.

By now the Italian industry itself was moribund but distinct efforts were made to revive it. Although these had some success in the period up to the First World War most of the later copies were made in Belgium where the part-lace tradition had survived through many changes in style since the 17th century.

As with other antique laces that were copied in this period, some close imitations were made, but many 19th-century examples are easily identifiable by their shapes,

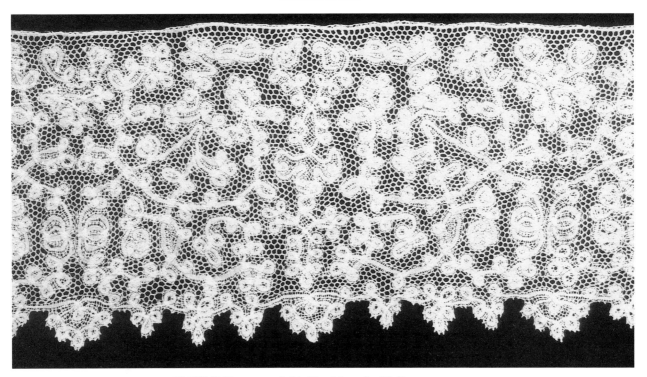

PLATE 86: Flounce, probably Flemish: early 18th C.
   Depth shown 16.5 cm (6.5 in)
   Pattern repeat 25 cm (9.5 in)
   Length shown 33 cm (13 in)
The scrolling pattern is very similar in style to that of the flounce
in Plate 81 but the tape is not continuous; the pattern is worked as
a part lace. This, and the looseness of working of the round mesh
ground, as well as the multitude of loops in the tape suggest that
this is probably of Flemish rather than North Italian origin.

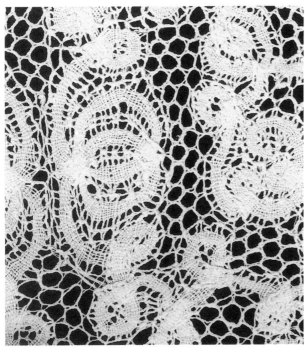

PLATE 87: Detail of Plate 86.

PLATE 88: Bertha collar: Belgian: about 1890–1900.
   Maximum outer diameter 60 cm (24 in)
   Inner diameter 17 cm (7 in)
The interest in antique laces at the end of the 19th century led to
many derivative designs as well as to direct copies. Here Italian
baroque motifs are arranged in a typical late 19th century circular
bertha but within the scalloped edge found in early 17th-century
laces or in French designs of about 1700.

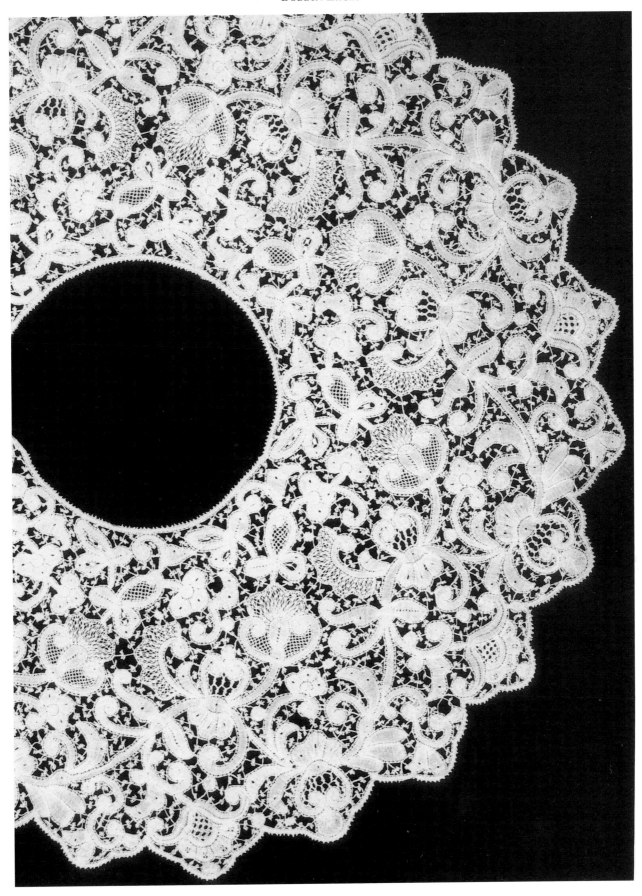

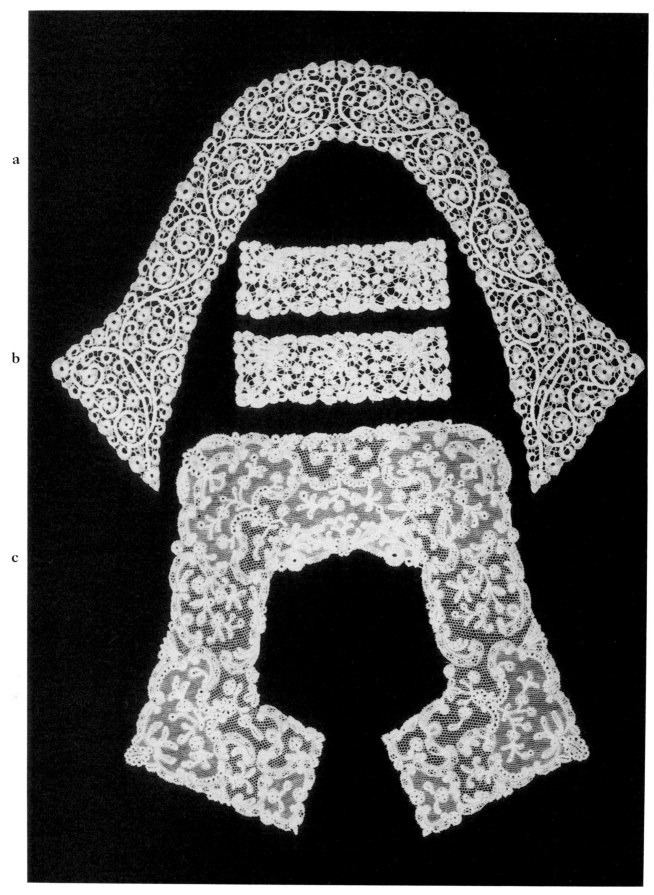

a

b

c

their mixture of styles from different periods, their thread, or their workmanship. One notable example is shown in Plate 88.

One new and specific imitation was introduced in about 1900 under the name 'rosaline' (see Plate 89). This was based primarily on the narrow, scrolling tape-like designs of Venetian needle and bobbin laces of about 1700 but some variants have more in common with Flemish laces derived from French designs of the period.

The French influence in Flemish part laces

The influence of French designs on Brussels needlepoints in the late 17th century was mentioned in an earlier chapter and their effect on her bobbin laces, and on those of neighbouring Flanders, will come as no surprise. The earliest laces derived from the new French classical style date from the 1680s or 1690s. In these, the sense of continuous movement in the preceding baroque style has gone and only the tiny scale and curving nature of its later motifs remain. The scattered branches, ideally suited to the part technique, are grouped about vertical axes centred on candelabra-like motifs and are joined by a bar or net ground. Even the smooth outlines of the earlier strong, baroque curves are broken by feathery leaves and buds which sprout in all directions.

The subsequent changes which occurred in this style are difficult to follow but in the 1700s the designs appear to have turned briefly from repeated symmetrical designs to asymmetric arrangements such as that illustrated in Plate 90b. The symmetry of the classical style may never have been abandoned entirely; certainly it is seen again in the early 18th century as the motifs gradually expanded to fill the space previously taken up by the ground.

By this time the fineness of the Brussels laces had distinguished them from the overall group of Flemish part laces and changes in design in the 18th century will be considered more fully in relation to this more fashionable lace. In general the poorer-quality laces, which were made in enormous flounces often for furnishing purposes, followed substantially the same trends, but often with some time lag because of the persistence of old designs in less organized industries. Many of these flounces, such as that in Plate 92, have in the past been attributed to Brabant a promise north and east of Brussels, but may equally well have been made in the smaller Flemish towns or perhaps even in England, by the East Devon industry.

PLATE 89:
a. Collar of Belgian rosaline lace: 1900–15.
    Maximum width 58 cm (23 in)
The design of this rosaline lace is very closely modelled on its Venetian predecessor (Plate 80); the collar shape is the obvious clue to its late date, but it is slightly less tightly worked and in a slightly coarser thread than the Venetian original. Rosaline laces is this style were known as 'Rosaline de fantaisie'.

b. Cuffs of Belgian rosaline lace: 1900–15.
    Depth 6 cm (2.3 in)
    Length 18 cm (7.2 in)

c. Collar of Belgian rosaline lace: 1900–15.
    Width 43 cm (17 in)
The designs of both the cuffs (b) and the collar (c) are more reminiscent of Flemish laces in the candelabra style than of the Italian baroque. The collar is grounded with needlepoint net of Alençon type (page 37) worked in two different thicknesses of thread and in two mesh sizes.

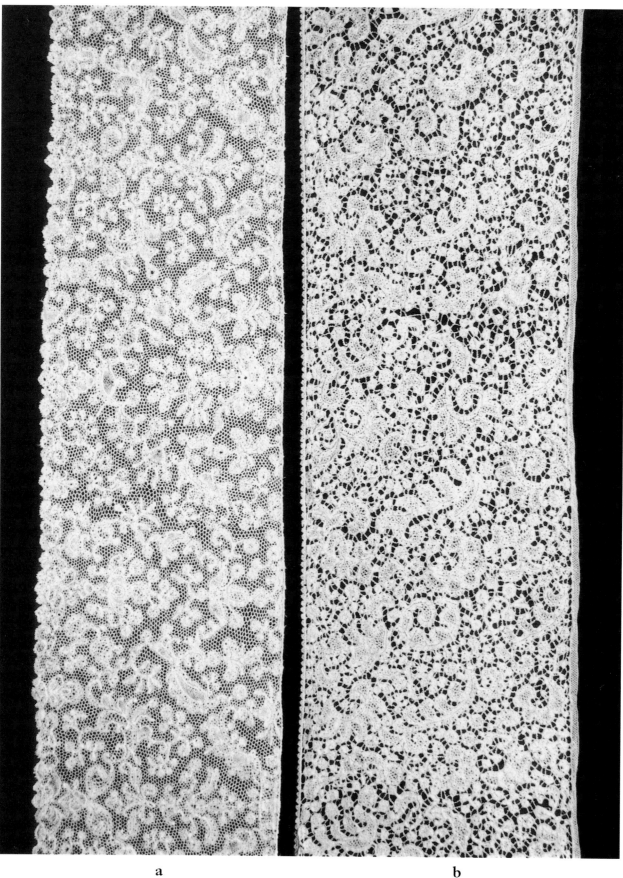

a   b

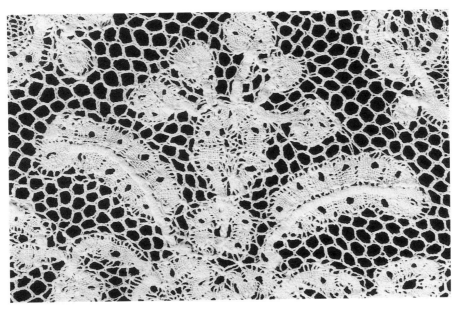

PLATE 91: detail of Plate 90*a*.
Note the loose working of the round Flemish ground and the
narrow band of clothwork forming the centres of the leaves: these
are raised over the surface and typify later Brussels bobbin laces.

PLATE 90:

a. Flemish flounce (possibly Brussels) with the round Flemish
mesh ground: 1690–1710.

   Depth 21 cm (8 in)

   Pattern repeat 54 cm (21.5 in)

   Length shown 71 cm (28 in)

This shows a typical example of what is known as the 'candelabra'
design, with its symmetrical groupings of motifs about
candelabra-like features. It appears to have been derived from the
French Bérainesque designs of point de France but is by no means
a direct copy.

b. Flemish flounce with a bar ground: 1700–20.

   Depth 24 cm (9.5 in)

   Pattern repeat 47 cm (18.5 in)

This design lacks the symmetry of the flounce above and the bud
and leaf motifs are on a slightly larger scale and more crowded,
indicating a slightly later date.

   The bar ground was largely superseded by net grounds in the
early 18th century but was still used occasionally even in the
second half of the century.

FIGURE 14: Man's cravat; about 1700.

In the 1670s there was a radical simplification of men's dress with
the introduction of the long, tight-fitting vest and coat. The rabat
collar (Figure 13) was gradually ousted by the cravat, a long strip of
linen which wrapped around the neck and tied at the front. It often
had rectangular lace panels at the ends which fell in graceful folds
at the neck.

PLATE 92: Flounce of a type formerly known as 'Brabant' but possibly made in Brabant or in Flanders: about 1740–60.

    Depth shown 57 cm (22.5 in)

    Width shown 81 cm (32 in)

    Full depth 60 cm (24 in)

    Pattern repeat 48 cm (19 in)

The naturalistic floral design of this flounce is completely different from the stylized designs in Plate 90 and follows the new trends introduced in the early 18th century and discussed in the needlepoint section and in the bobbin sections which follow. It is made in a far coarser, poorer-quality thread and with much looser workmanship than the related Brussels laces; this enabled such large pieces to be made comparatively quickly and cheaply.

PLATE 93: Collar: about 1880–1890.

    Diameter of neck opening 14 cm (5.5 in)

    Maximum width 38 cm (15 in)

This collar is of a type known as 'Russian' lace despite the fact that it was made in western Europe. Its style followed that of eastern European laces which were still being made in convoluted designs developed from the North Italian tape laces of the 18th century (Plate 81).

    Many of the true Russian laces were enlivened by the inclusion of animals, birds and human figures or coloured threads in the designs but were largely made for the home market and are rarely found in Western collections.

BRUSSELS, INCLUDING MIXED BOBBIN AND NEEDLEPOINT LACES

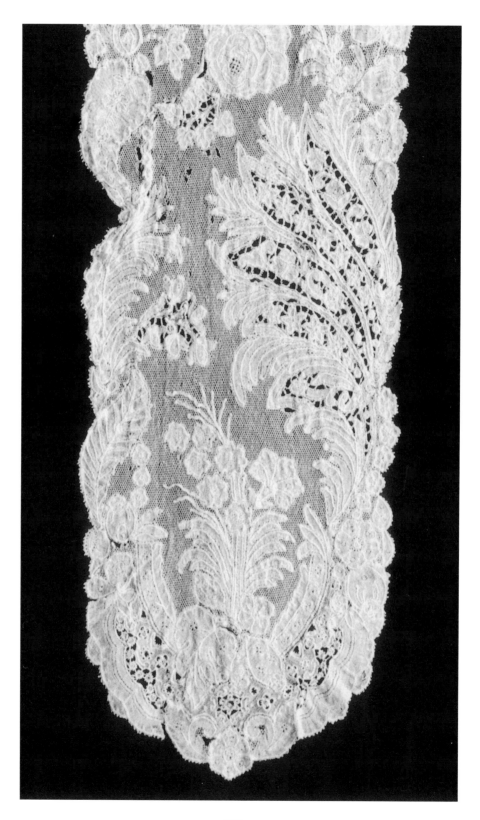

Characteristics

1. Part lace.

2. Pattern areas mainly in clothwork but with some half stitch.

3. Right and wrong sides differ.

   a. Right side has raised work in the form of narrow bands of clothwork (Plate 95) or bundles of threads (Plate 107) outlining some edges and features within the design.

   b. Wrong side often has groups of threads passing loosely across it from one area of working to another.

4. A gimp thread is sometimes incorporated in 19th-century designs.

5. Needlework is often incorporated as complete motifs, as decorative fillings and spots, or as the ground.

6. Designs are generally well organized and drawn.

7. Spots or tiny sprigs are often scattered over the ground in 19th-century examples.

8. Grounds:

   a. Bobbin-made brides often decorated with picots were common in the early to mid-18th century and after about 1850.

   b. Vrai-drochel bobbin ground (Figure 15) – elongated hexagonal mesh with two sides of four plaited threads and four sides of two twisted threads – was common from the early 18th century to mid-19th century

   c. Point de gaze needlepoint ground after about 1850 (Figure 10, page 53).

   d. Alençon needlepoint ground, often with coarse meshes, after about 1850 (Figure 5, page 37).

   e. Needle-made brides in the coarse Duchesse lace (see Plate 107).

   f. Machine net used from the early 19th century onwards.

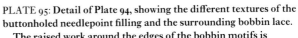

PLATE 95: Detail of Plate 94, showing the different textures of the buttonholed needlepoint filling and the surrounding bobbin lace.

The raised work around the edges of the bobbin motifs is worked first and then the cloth stitch is worked over them. The motifs are thus worked face-down and the lace maker would not have seen the finished result until the lace was lifted from the pricking.

PLATE 94: Brussels mixed bobbin and needlepoint lappet: 1745–60.

    Width 8.5 cm (3.3 in)

    Length shown 20 cm (8 in)

    Full length 60 cm (24 in)

This lappet shows a style between those of the lappets *b* and *c* in Plate 97 (page 108). Note the contrasting effect of the fine drochel ground in the centre and the open bar ground in the feathery leaves which spring from the edge; these form a pattern resembling a typical rococo shell motif.

Although described as a mixed lace, the needlepoint here forms only a small crescent of filling stitches in the end of the lappet (see detail, Plate 95).

Lappets formed part of a woman's head-dress, as indicated in Figure 6 (page 40). In the late 17th century they were narrow, often with edges of tiny scallops. They then became wider and straight-edged, often narrowing slightly towards the end. By 1730 the straight edge was softening into slight waves but a rounded end and more wavy-edged form had already been introduced. By 1740 the rounded end with a wavy edge was usual but in the later 18th century the straight edges returned.

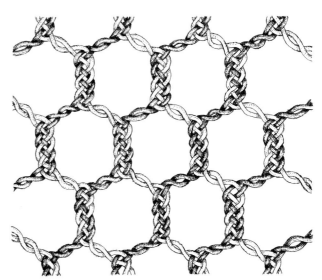

FIGURE 15: The vrai drochel ground.

a

b

c

d

Points to watch

The vrai-drochel ground is very similar to the Mechlin ground (see page 145) but Brussels plaits are longer by one half stitch.

East Devon (Honiton) lace is technically very similar to Brussels bobbin lace but much less care was taken over design and consistency of workmanship than in Brussels laces. Eighteenth-century East Devon lace is sometimes identified by the poorer quality thread used; this can give the lace a slightly fuzzy appearance and softer feel than given by the firmly twisted, long staple Flemish thread. The drochel ground was sometimes worked in different directions within an English lace whereas Brussels workers normally worked it consistently in one direction throughout a lace.

PLATE 96: Group of edgings
Length shown 34 cm (13.5 in)

a.   About 1700.
   Depth 8.0 cm (3.2 in)
   No clear pattern repeat
By 1700 the Italian baroque designs had degenerated into confused designs such as this but an interesting feature is the formation of the tape on the surface, around the edges of the half-stitch pattern areas. This probably developed into the raised work of later Brussels laces.

b.   About 1700–10.
   Depth 8.4 cm (3.3 in); design altered
Compare this piece with the flounces in Plate 90 (page 100). Its design has the symmetry of flounce (a) but the scale of the motifs in relation to the depth of the lace and their style are more in keeping with flounce (b).

c.   About 1745–60.
   Depth 7.5 cm (3.0 in)
   Pattern repeat 60 cm (23.5 in)
The light-hearted feel of this design, with its scattering of birds and butterflies, is typical of the rococo style. Some fillings are closely similar to needlepoint fillings in appearance; needlepoints were again popular in this period and various features were borrowed by bobbin laces.

d.   Edging with shaped ends: about 1820–30.
   Depth 6.5 cm (2.5 in)
   Full length 99 cm (39 in); no exact pattern repeat
Stylistically this lace could almost be of about 1770, but the working is too precise, the fillings too organized for an 18th-century piece. It must be 19th century, but pre-1850 when the drochel ground had almost died out: it dates from the period when designs were just becoming free of the constraints of the classical period.

History

The history of Brussels lace in the 17th century is obscure, partly because of the confusion that has arisen over the term 'Point d'Angleterre'. This is a name which has long been attributed to the finest Brussels laces. It was certainly in use in the early to mid-18th century, when records clearly state that lace of this name was made in Brussels, but it was also used in the late 17th century with no categorical indication of origin.

Arguments currently abound over whether this term was first applied to an English lace later copied in Brussels or to a Brussels lace made largely for the English market, with various amusing variations such as, 'It must have been intended for the French market because of the use of the French language.' The question is not without interest but is of little help to us in distinguishing lace made in Brussels from the technically similar lace of East Devon, generally known as Honiton lace.

What is fairly certain is that Brussels was one of the centres for the manufacture of Flemish part laces in the Italian baroque style in the second half of the 17th century. We have followed the gradual degeneration of this style from the bold designs of the 1650s to 1670s (pages 92–5) to the rather fussy style of about 1700 but at this point an interesting development occurred. The crowded designs of this period, with their narrow, curving and branching stems and tiny flower buds, are often found in a form of tape lace as seen in Plate 96a. Here the tape, which is not pre-made but is worked with bobbins on the pillow, is looped over itself and forms a raised edge on the surface around the edges of tiny areas of cloth stitch or half stitch. This may be the start of the raised outline of Brussels lace which was to become a major characteristic in the 18th and 19th centuries. Raised leaf centres, however, are also seen in the French-style laces of about the same date (Plates 90 and 91).

Both the laces shown in Plate 90 are flounces and were probably made for furnishing use since there was little call for lace on this scale for dress in the early years of the 18th century. Much finer laces in this style and technique were also made, however; an example is shown in Plate 96b. Laces of this type, with their clear designs and good workmanship and, more particularly, their incredibly fine, firmly-twisted thread, are among the first attributable with any certainty to Brussels. Despite this new style, the Brussels industry went through a difficult period during the first two decades of the 18th century as fashion favoured trimmings of plain lawn and gauze. A new impetus was needed and it came in the form of the 'bizarre' designs which had been introduced into French woven silks at the very end of the 17th century.

The belated effect of these designs on French and Brussels needlepoints in the 1720s and 1730s has already been seen but the full impact occurred in the 1710s upon Flemish bobbin laces and particularly those of Valenciennes and Brussels. The new style was in the baroque tradition, with bold designs full of vigour and movement: the large-

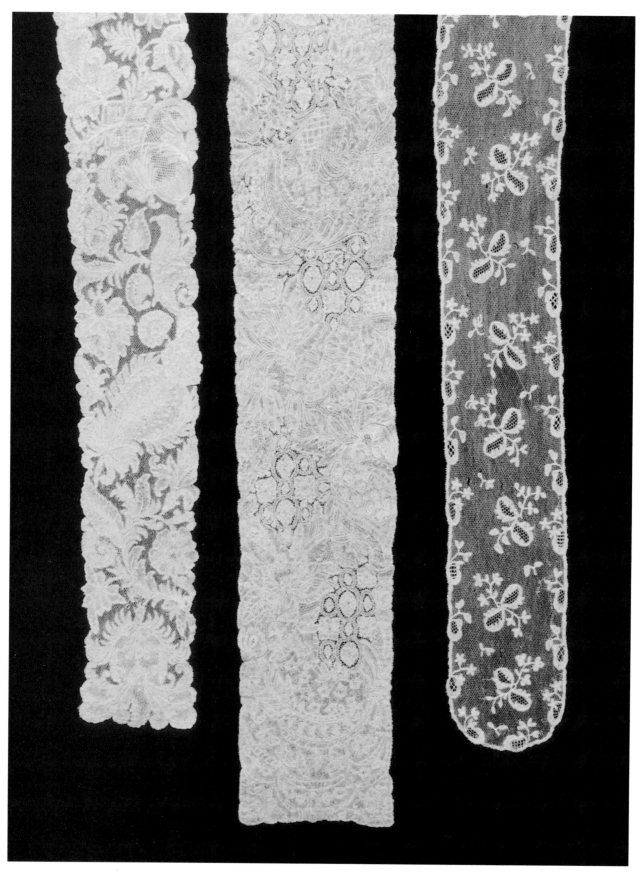

PLATE 97:

a. (*centre*). Probably Brussels but possibly East Devon (Honiton): about 1720–30.

    Length shown 48 cm (19 in)

    Full length 65 cm (26 in)

This exemplifies the rich patterning of the 'bizarre' designs but is not quite as accomplished as many of the contemporary Valenciennes and Brussels designs. The thread and workmanship are extremely fine but the use of raised work is a little haphazard.

b. (*left*). Brussels: about 1730–35.

    Length shown 43 cm (17 in)

    Full length 53 cm (21 in)

c. (*right*). Brussels: about 1780–90.

    Length shown 44 cm (17.2 in)

    Full length 72 cm (28.5 in)

PLATE 98: Veil: Brussels bobbin motifs applied to drochel ground: 1820–30.

    Pattern repeat 10 cm (4 in)

    Pattern depth 21 cm (8.5 in)

    Full width 141 cm (56 in)

    Full length 118 cm (47 in)

The edging of pointed leaves continues around the entire veil which was probably worn draped over the shoulders with the top gathered and tied or pinned into the hair.

    Edgings of tiny points were a common alternative to absolutely straight edges from the 1790s through to the 1820s. Small, rounded scallops had also appeared by this time; these broadened into fuller scallops in the 1830s before dwindling to a slightly wavy headside in the 1840s, rather as they had in the early 17th century (see Plate 100 for detail).

FIGURE 16: Woman with bonnet veil; about 1820.
The shape of bonnets varied enormously in the 19th century. In general the long narrow shape of the 1800s was transformed by the late 1820s and 1830s into a bonnet with a flaring brim which gradually shrank through the 1840s until, in the 1860s, it became simply a small cap worn on the back of the head. Throughout this period bonnets were worn with veils which usually had a draw string along the upper edge by which they were attached to the bonnet; the size and shape of the veil varied with that of the bonnet.

PLATE 100:
a. (*above*). Detail of the edge of the veil in Plate 99, showing the bobbin-made motifs applied to a machine-made net which has been cut away behind the open flower centres. The spot-filling is needle-made.

Note the use of the thick gimp thread to outline the flower petals and the raised work on the leaves and stems.

b. (*below*). Detail of the edge of the veil in Plate 98 showing the bobbin-made motifs applied to the bobbin-made drochel ground.

The clothwork is more more loosely worked in both these examples than in the 18th-century laces. This is a common, but not invariable feature of the 19th-century laces (see Plate 96d).

PLATE 99: Bonnet veil: Brussels bobbin motifs applied to a machine-made net: 1840–50.
Width 110 cm (44 in)
Length 89 cm (35 in)
There are 5 pattern repeats.

Unlike the veil in Plate 98, this has a draw string along its upper edge for fastening the veil to a bonnet.

Compare the typical, rather tenuous floral edging pattern with that of the contemporary veil in Plate 39 and the sprig design to the earlier examples in Plates 67 and 145.

scale motifs of exotic fruits and flowerheads, feathery leaves and geometric shapes show the influence both of the far and of the near East but their treatment is wholly different from that of the 17th-century Italian baroque. Now the motifs are crowded together in abstract patterns, with shapes bounded by odd combinations of angles and re-entrant curves and juxtaposed with leafy sprays. The strongly diagonal movement of the wider, woven silks is translated into a movement to and fro across the narrower lace designs and the vibrant colours of the silks are echoed in the rich patterning of the lace motifs with filling stitches and scatterings of tinier motifs.

The result is seen in the lappet in Plate 97a. Here the motifs are so crowded that the lace is almost opaque but this again suited the fashion of the day; the desire for lack of ostentation is catered for by the fact that the pattern is scarcely discernible at distances of more than a few feet while the need to display wealth is satisfied by the extreme intricacy seen at close quarters.

Although little is known of designers in the lace industry itself and few laces are dated, there is a remarkable similarity between these densely patterned laces and the woven silks of the early 18th century, for which dated records are available. This enables the better-quality laces made by manufacturers who employed the best designers or who bought in the latest designs, to be dated to within a decade. This

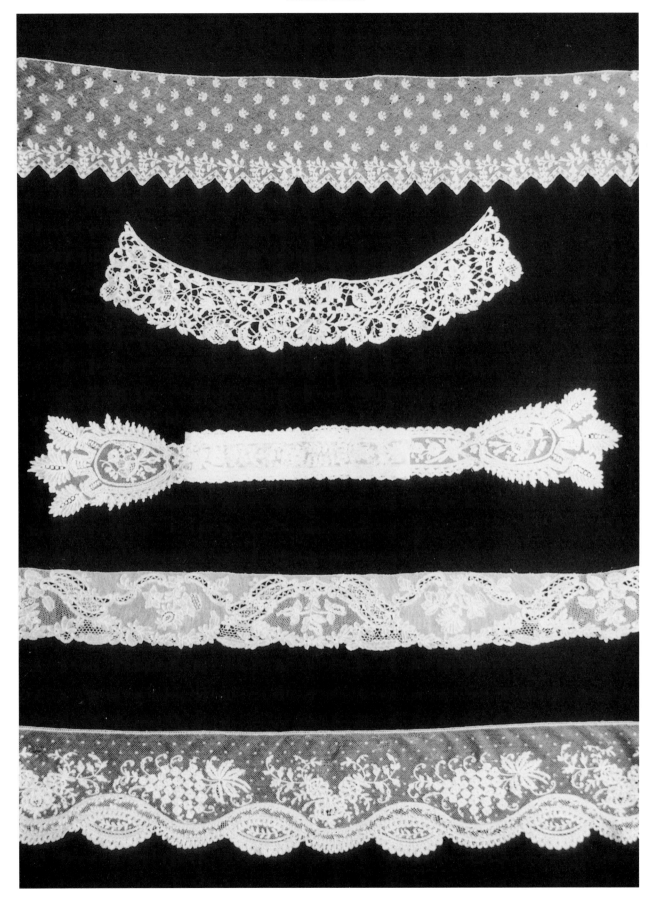

PLATE 102: Edging of mixed
Brussels needlepoint and
bobbin lace with the point de
gaze ground: about 1860–80.
Depth 4.5 cm (1.8 in)
Pattern repeat 4.3 cm (1.7 in)
The central flower head and
its leaves are in bobbin lace;
the ring fillings and the rest of
the lace are in needlepoint.

PLATE 101:

a. Edging of bobbin appliqué on drochel ground: about 1815–25.
Probably Brussels, but some design irregularities suggest it might
be Honiton.
   Maximum depth 10 cm (4 in)
   Length shown 56 cm (22 in)

b. Collar of Brussels guipure with bobbin-made brides: about
1850–60.
   Depth 6 cm (2.3 in)
   Full length of inside edge 38 cm (15 in)

c. Tie of Brussels bobbin appliqué on machine-made net: about
1870–90.
   Maximum width of ends 9 cm (3.5 in)
   Full length 96 cm (38 in)
Shaped accessories like this, with a narrow centre broadening into
bulbous or splayed ends, are thought to have been worn around
the neck and are usually called 'ties' although they could equally
well have been used as lappets as occasion demanded.

d. Edging of Brussels bobbin lace with the Alençon needlepoint
ground: probably about 1840–60, but possibly later.
   Maximum depth 7.5 cm (3.0 in)
   Pattern repeat 26.5 cm (10.5 in)
This edging is an almost direct copy of an 18th-century rococo
design but the thread, the use of the Alençon ground and a less
delicate treatment of the design betray its 19th-century origin.

e. Edging of Brussels bobbin appliqué on machine-made net:
about 1855–70.
   Maximum depth 11 cm (4.5 in)
   Pattern repeat 27 cm (11 in)

cannot be said, however, for the mass of poorer-quality
laces, whether made in Brussels, or in the minor lace-making
regions of Europe where links with France were not so
strong.

Gradually, as the bizarre designs were modified, more
naturalistic European flowers were introduced and the odd
cartouche shapes became less dominant.

The early designs left little room for any ground between
the densely-packed motifs but, by 1730, designs were again
opening out. The rhythmic movement was still retained but
floral or leafy sprigs gained more importance and curved
into well-defined spaces bordered by patterned strapwork,
cartouches of fancy fillings or by trails of the leaves
themselves. Display was again acceptable in dress and the
bride ground of the earlier period (Plate 96b) was largely
replaced by a lighter, net ground which gave a greater
contrast with the pattern. This new ground was the 'drochel'
or 'vrai drochel' ground which had been known as a filling
stitch from the 17th century but was to assume an ever-
increasing role in Brussels laces in the 18th century.

As designs grew lighter in the 1740s, they also became
more light-hearted with the introduction of rococo scrolls
and shell ornamentation, birds and insects (Plate 96c).
Chinoiserie motifs such as pagodas, pavilions and figures in
Chinese dress which had occasionally been seen in designs
throughout the earlier part of the century became more
common.

The rococo style was to last into the 1760s and early 1770s
but we have already followed its decline in the French laces
of Alençon and Argentan. The only major innovation in the
Brussels industry was in the grounding of the motifs. While

PLATE 104: Detail of Plate 103 showing the differing textures of the clothwork and raised work in the bobbin-made leaf and the needlepoint rose.

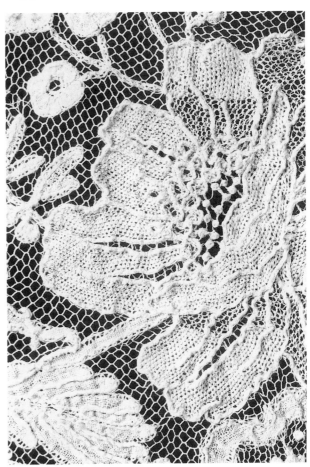

FIGURE 17: Woman in mid-19th century evening dress. The evening neckline for dresses in the 1840s to 1860s was low cut and often trimmed with a wide collar known as a 'bertha'. This was often of lace and usually had an opening down the centre front of the dress. In the mid-19th century the bertha was generally boat-shaped, like the neckline, whereas in the 1890s and 1900s berthas were usually circular.

Berthas were often made *en suite* with lace lappets, sleeves and other dress trimmings, possibly including wide flounces for the huge skirts of the crinoline period. The flounces might be made in graduated widths with matching patterns for wear in tiers on the skirt.

PLATE 103: Flounce of mixed Brussels needlepoint and bobbin lace applied to a machine-made net: about 1850–75.
Maximum depth 36 cm (14 in)
Pattern repeat 68 cm (27 in)
Length shown 76 cm (31 in)

these were closely spaced, they were arranged on a pattern and the drochel ground was worked between and around them and the threads of the ground are often seen carried across the backs of the motifs, as in the drochel-grounded Brussels needlepoints. In the later examples with linear patterns and scattered motifs, the ground was made separately and the design applied to it. In practice, the ground was worked in narrow widths, from about 1 to 2.5 cm ($\frac{1}{2}$ to 1 in) wide, and these were subsequently joined edge to edge to form larger panels. Well before 1800, the joining technique, with a stitch known as point de racroc, was so well developed that the joins were invisible although, with subsequent wear, they now appear as breaks in the lace.

In the late 18th century the Brussels bobbin lace industry suffered the same decline as its needlepoint. The gossamer-fine drochel net suited the fashions and was made in large panels patterned with neo-classical designs for use as aprons, fichus and other accessories but much cheaper fabrics served the same purposes. Only Brussels' name for quality kept the industry alive.

In the early 19th century, Napoleon's patronage was of some assistance and the continuance of the industry is shown by the number of large veils (Plate 98) which still exist from the 1820s and 1830s but fashion was not to turn to

the fuller designs, most effective in this lace, until the 1840s. By this time it was no longer economic to make net by hand but the possibilities of machine-made nets had been discovered. The manufacture of the drochel ground ceased by about 1850 for all but the most special orders or exhibition pieces.

The 1840s saw the start of a new boom in the lace trade. With the industrialization of Europe and the wider spread of wealth, more people could afford the lace which fashion now dictated should be worn. Those who could not afford the more prestigious hand-made laces could choose from a growing supply of machine laces or from the cheaper hand-made guipures which were now coming on to the market.

The Brussels industry was well placed to take advantage of the mood. Its manufacturers had close links with Paris where the French court under Louis Napoleon and, more specifically his wife, Eugénie, again led the fashion in Europe. Together with the new needlepoint, point de gaze (pages 52–6), Brussels application laces on machine-made net were among the most sought after in Europe and were to remain so for the rest of the century. They were particularly required in wide flounces for the crinoline dresses of the 1850s and 1860s and as large squares, of up to 2 metres (2 yards), for wedding veils and shawls. Confusingly they were sold under the name 'Application d'Angleterre'.

The design changes in these laces were limited but followed the same trends as those already seen in Brussels point de gaze. Indeed, the best of these application laces combined the needle and bobbin techniques. This was not a new departure for the Brussels lacemakers; 18th-century Brussels bobbin laces had often incorporated small amounts of needlepoint while the 18th-century needlepoints were often grounded with the bobbin drochel net. In the late 19th century, their combination was taken to new extremes. In the most expensive fabrics, the mixture of needle and bobbin motifs was even grounded with the hand-made point de gaze net; the name 'point d'Angleterre' was used once more.

The application laces were only one form of Brussels lace. The growing interest in all-over patterns and the reintro-

duction of guipures in the 1840s also led to the return of Brussels laces grounded with bars, or brides. In some cases the lace was of the same fine quality, made in the same fine thread as the application laces; an example is shown in Plate 101b. More often a much heavier thread was used and the result was a new lace, called 'Duchesse' in honour of the Duchess of Brabant, subsquently Queen of the Belgians.

The Duchesse laces are generally grouped into two classes; those including needlework fillings or insets of point de gaze lace which are known as 'Brussels Duchesse' and those without needlework which are known as 'Bruges Duchesse'. Usually the former are of finer quality but to what extent they were actually made in the capital is uncertain. By the latter part of the 19th century many of the Belgian lace manufacturers had moved their main premises out of Brussels to smaller towns such as Bruges and Ghent which had long lace-making traditions of their own. Records show that much of the cheaper lace was made here while even the fine motifs for the application laces were made at Binche and other centres.

The collapse of the French Second Empire in 1870 and the concurrent changes in fashion were not disastrous for the better quality Brussels laces which were still much in demand for wedding trousseaux but they did affect the cheaper guipures. The revival of the lace industry in the 1880s included the copying of antique laces and led to one last innovation: the modification of Duchesse guipures to form the lace known as 'rosaline' already seen in Plate 89.

The First World War effectively brought an end to the Belgian lace industry but lacemakers can still occasionally be seen in the streets of Bruges and the thriving lace school attracts new pupils every year.

PLATE 105: **Fan of mixed Brussels bobbin and needlepoint lace applied to a machine-made net: about 1890–1900.**
Full width 67 cm (26.5 in)
Depth of lace 22 cm (8.5 in)
The asymmetric floral design interspersed with scrolls and cartouches of fancy fillings is typical of the revived rococo style of the late 19th century: it is fuller and more assured than the 1840 rococo designs and is not a direct copy of an 18th-century design, unlike the design in Plate 101d. Large, semi-circular fans are typical of the late 19th century.

PLATE 106:

a. Collar of Brussels (mixed) Duchesse: 1880–1910.
    Maximum width 57 cm (22.5 in)

b. Woman's jabot of Bruges bobbin Duchesse attached to
machine-made net: about 1900.
    Maximum width 13 cm (5.2 in)
Jabots of this type were worn with the high-necked dresses of the
late 19th century and into the 20th century.

c. Collar of Brussels (mixed) Duchesse: late 19th century.
    Length of neck edge 22.5 cm (9.5 in)
    Centre depth 5 cm (2 in)

d. Edging of Brussels (mixed) Duchesse: late 19th–20th century.
    Depth 8.5 cm (3.3 in)
    Pattern repeat 16 cm (6.5 in)

PLATE 107: **Detail of the collar in Plate 106a. Note the needlepoint brides and the raised petals of the needlepoint rose. The bobbin raised-work consists of bundles of threads – the more difficult cloth stitch raised work is rarely found in Duchesse laces, even in good-quality examples like this.**

PLATE 108: **Detail of a Brussels duchesse lace (*bottom*) with a chemical machine-lace copy (*top*). To the naked eye, this machine copy is extremely similar to a bobbin lace; only the confused, rather fuzzy structure of the bars and net ground give an immediate indication of its machine origin. (See Plate 173 for a further example and explanation of chemical lace.)**

EAST DEVON (HONITON)

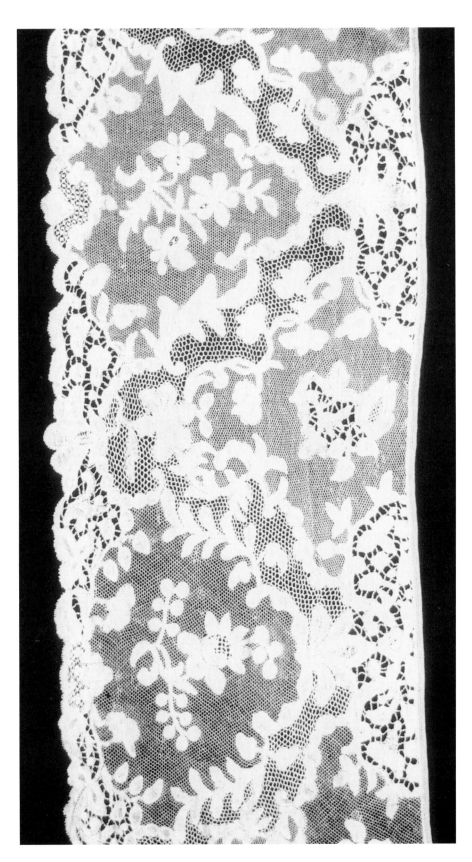

Characteristics

1. Part lace.

2. Pattern areas mainly in clothwork but with some half stitch.

3. Right and wrong sides differ.

    a. Right side has raised work in the form of narrow bands of clothwork or bundles of threads outlining some edges and features within the design.

    b. Wrong side often has groups of threads passing loosely across it from one area of working to another.

4. A gimp thread is often incorporated (mainly in the 19th-century designs).

5. Designs are less skilfully drawn than continental designs, even in better-quality examples; in poorer pieces, leaves, flowers and other motifs are scattered indiscriminately.

6. Nineteenth-century designs often include stylized cabbage roses and leadwork fillings (Plate 117).

7. Grounds:

    a. Bobbin-made brides, often decorated with picots (common in the early to mid-18th century and again after about 1850).

    b. Vrai drochel bobbin net (Figure 18). Elongated hexagonal mesh with two sides of four plaited threads and four sides of two twisted threads (common from the early 18th century to the early 19th century).

    c. Alençon needlepoint net, usually with coarse meshes, after about 1850 (Figure 5, page 37).

    d. Needle-made brides after about 1850.

    e. Machine-made net used from the early 19th century.

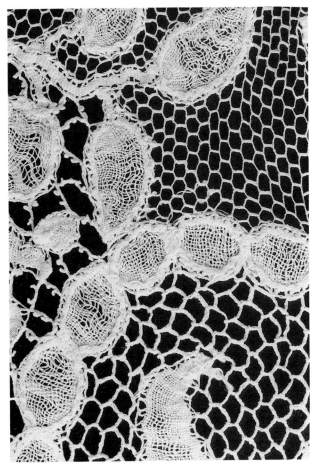

PLATE 110: **Detail of Plate 109 showing the drochel ground and a looped filling stitch which at first glance looks like a needlepoint filling but is, in fact, bobbin-made.**

PLATE 109: **Devon flounce: about 1750–70.**
    Depth 29 cm (11.5 in)
    Pattern repeat 69 cm (27 in)
    Length shown 60 cm (23.5 in)
The thread and workmanship in this piece are much better than in the flounce in Plate 92 but the areas of cloth stitch and half stitch are more loosely worked and there is less raised work than in the narrower edgings and lappets of Plates 111 and 112.

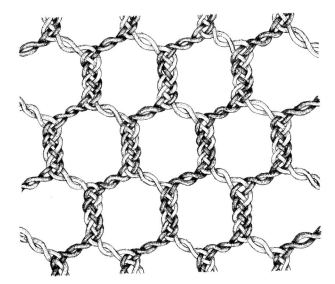

FIGURE 18: **The vrai drochel ground.**

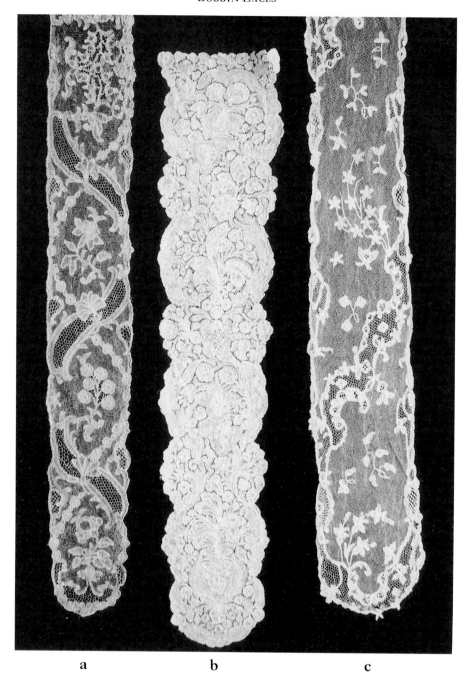

a   b   c

PLATE 111: **Group of lappets.**
a. (*centre*). About 1725–35.
   Full length 57 cm (22.5 in)
This lappet has the same density of design as the lappet in Plate
97*a* but its more floral character exemplifies a later stage in the
development of the 'bizarre' designs. The scalloped edge and
rounded end of the lappet are also later features.

b. (*left*). About 1750–60.
   Length shown 58.5 cm (23 in)
   Full length 53 cm (21 in)

c. (*right*). About 1760–70.
   Length shown 58.5 cm (23 in)
   Full length 77 cm (30 in)

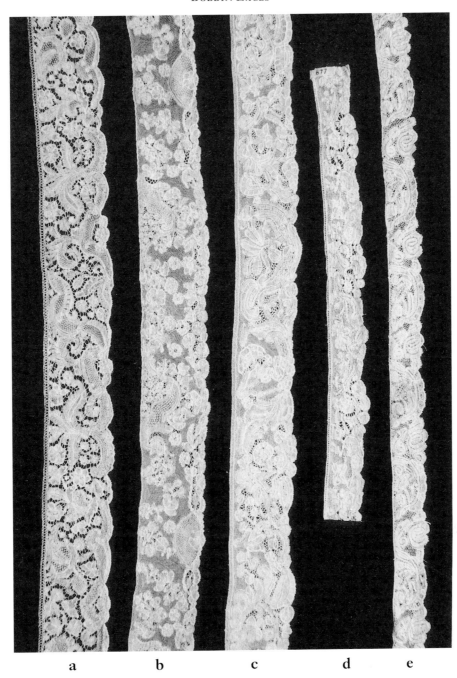

a   b   c   d   e

PLATE 112: **Group of 18th-century edgings.**
   Length shown 57 cm (22.5 in)
   Depth
      a, b, c 7 cm (2.7 in)
      d, e 3.7 cm (1.5 in)

a.   About 1710–15

b.   About 1740–60

c to e.   Late 18th C

Edgings (*b*) to (*e*) show stages which might occur in the deterioration of a design worked on the same pricking over many years or even decades. This deterioration may be due in part to the misinterpretation of a pricking which is, after all, simply an array of holes and in part to the pinholes becoming enlarged with use so that motifs become distorted. Thus flowerheads comprising a ring of distinct petals around a circular centre in (*b*) could become less defined and end up as the whorls seen in (*e*). Lace in designs like that of example (*e*) are, unfortunately, comparatively common and have long been illustrated as the only lace made in Devon in the 18th century.

Points to watch

East Devon lace is technically very similar to Brussels bobbin lace and better quality examples of English work can be very difficult to distinguish from Brussels laces. The mass of East Devon lace is, however, poorly designed and easy to recognize.

The thread used can be a distinguishing factor. In the 18th century, the English thread was whiter and softer (less firmly twisted) than the Brussels thread but the difference this gives to the feel and appearance of a lace has in many cases been lost due to wear and washing over the centuries. Imported Flemish thread was occasionally used in England although it was extremely expensive and hard to obtain.

In the 19th century even the poorest-quality Honiton laces were made in relatively fine thread. In Belgium, on the other hand, the finer threads were reserved for the better quality laces while the poorer Duchesse guipures were made in coarse threads.

History

Various records show that, by the late 17th century, lace-making was well established in the East Devon villages around Honiton but what is not so clear is the type and quality of the lace that was made. Celia Fiennes, a visitor to the area in the late 17th century, remarked merely that lace made there was as fine as Flanders lace but did not wash so well, and records in the early 18th century are no more specific. By the late 18th century the Devon lace-makers were certainly making part bobbin laces similar to those of Brussels and from comments such as Celia Fiennes', it is perhaps fair to assume that this was so in the earlier period. The problem with washing may well have been due to the poorer-quality English thread and is one factor in the attribution of the edging in Plate 112*a* to Devon.

What is surprising in Celia Fiennes' remarks is her comment on the quality of the English lace. This is not to suggest that Devon workers were incapable of the high standards set by continental workers; but in the 18th century the Devon and Brussels industries operated in an entirely different manner. In Brussels the manufacturers were based in a major city with strong links with Paris and the French court, their major market. They controlled large workforces to whom they supplied thread and patterns and whose work they could oversee. They hired their own designers or imported designs from France where designers were trained at the government-run school.

In Devon there was no such organization. Many of the cottagers bought their own thread and worked their own patterns repeatedly. Others were supplied with thread and patterns by local dealers but it appears that no one manufacturer controlled a large body of workers who worked for him alone. Devon was also remote from London, its major market, and even here the English aristocracy, who spent much of the year on their country estates, were not so fashion-conscious as their French counterparts whose lives were spent at court. In Devon there was thus little incentive to control the quality of workmanship, to train specialist designers, or even to buy in new designs.

The major problem then with much of the Devon lace was in its design, or rather lack of it, and in a rather haphazard attitude to workmanship which led to the drochel ground being worked in different directions in the same piece, to the random use of filling stitches and raised work and to the combination of motifs worked by different people, to totally different standards, in a single article. New designs were, of course, introduced, as shown by the examples in Plates 109 to 113, but even the better examples are distinguished by a certain poverty in the drawing and a general lack of sophistication. Another problem was the reworking of old patterns which may not have been fully understood in the first place; the results of this are shown in Plate 112.

In previous chapters we have seen how the changes in fashion at the end of the 18th century led to the abandonment of densely-patterned laces suited to the part-lace technique. The drop in demand for Devon lace was felt particularly keenly because of the recent loss of Devon's other major market, after London. This was the USA which, with independence, was freed from the restrictions of being obliged to trade with Britain.

By 1800, of the thousands of lace makers in Devon a decade or so earlier, all but a few hundred had turned to other means of earning a living.

The early decades of the 19th century saw little improvement in the situation, despite the move of Heathcoat's machine-net factory from Nottingham to Tiverton in 1816. This provided a cheap foundation for the new Honiton application laces which considerably quickened the making of large items, such as veils and stoles, but even Queen Adelaide's order of Honiton lace could do little to promote the industry while fashion was against it.

By the beginning of Victoria's reign it was only with difficulty that enough workers could be found in and around

PLATE 113: Group of edgings: length shown 33 cm (13 in): *a* to *c* late 18th C. None of these 18th-century edgings is of very good quality and their designs are hard to date with any accuracy.

a. About 1750–70.
    Design incomplete; depth 7.5 cm (3.0 in)

b. About 1760–80.
    Pattern repeat 38 cm (15 in); depth 6.0 cm (2.0 in)

c. About 1775–1800.
    Pattern repeat 32 cm (12.5 in); depth 7.2 cm (2.9 in)

d. Early 19th century; about 1830–50.
    Pattern repeat 6.5 cm (2.6 in); depth 12.5 cm (5.0 in)
The repeated flowerhead forming a scalloped edge was a recurrent theme in 1830s designs but I have seen this carnation in a number of Honiton laces, often of clearly later date.

a

b

c

d

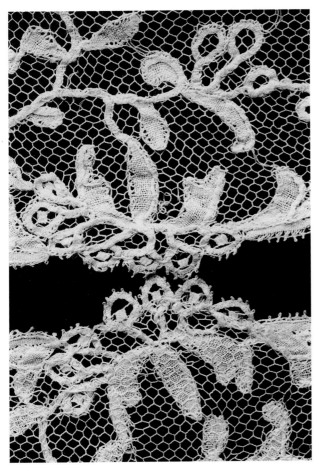

PLATE 115: Detail of the stole in Plate 114 showing the right side above and the wrong side below.

The cloth-stitch pattern is tightly worked and has good raised edges; this is typical of Honiton laces from the early 19th century before the lace boom of the 1850s caused a rapid deterioration in standards.

A gimp outlining thread is incorporated in the design and a Honiton leadwork filling (square spot) is seen in the edge motif.

PLATE 114: Stole of Honiton lace applied to a machine-made net: about 1840–50.

Width 35 cm (14 in)

Full length of stole 220 cm (88 in)

Length of patterned end 47 cm (18.5 in)

The arrangement of an asymmetric floral design within a triangular shape is typical of the 1840s, as is the weak, straggly nature of the flower sprigs. The similarity of the border design to that of the contemporary Brussels border in Plate 99 will be apparent but the Brussels design is better drawn and more orderly.

the little East Devon fishing village of Beer to complete an order for a flounce and matching trimmings of a quality suitable for a dress for the Sovereign. These pieces, supplemented with a veil, were subsequently worn at Queen Victoria's wedding and later at the christenings and weddings of many of her children.

The continuance of royal patronage in subsequent years, together with the reawakened desire for opulent designs suited to the Honiton technique, brought about the revival of the industry. The contemporary interest in guipure laces also saw the return of the bar-grounded lace. This was the start of a new boom and, for a short while, the fame of Honiton lace spread even to the continent. Copies of the new guipure were made at Mirecourt in Lorraine and to some extent in Belgium. Here cross-fertilization with the local 'duchesse' laces resulted in many hybrid versions whose origin is now almost impossible to distinguish.

The success of the industry in the 1850s and 1860s without any strong organization to sustain it was the main cause of its downfall. In order to satisfy the enormous demand for Honiton lace, the majority of workers lowered their standards and quickened their production. The difficult cloth stitch raised-work was replaced by bundles of threads loosely bound to the surface or omitted altogether. Such rudimentary designs as there had been were soon abandoned in favour of agglomerations of unrelated motifs or, at worst, an indeterminate mass of squiggles and curls often called 'slugs and snails'. Even the poorest of the laces shown in Plate 118 is not as bad as much of the produce of this period.

To put all the blame on the workers would be unfair. They were working long hours to scrape a living in the teeth of machine competition and were exploited by the many unscrupulous dealers who acted as agents for the sale of the lace in London and other cities. Only a very few establishments such as that of Mrs Treadwin in Exeter and John Tucker in Branscombe were concerned to maintain standards of quality and workmanship.

When the slump came in the 1870s, Devon's lacemakers were again forced into other forms of employment. Many of the Branscombe workers turned to a form of tape lace which we have already seen (pages 62–3) while Mrs Treadwin's workers were taught to repair and re-order antique laces which were becoming ever more popular. Even the 17th-century Venetian needlepoints were included in their repertoire.

When the final lace revival came in the late 1880s a few lacemakers returned to the industry but the lace schools which had provided new blood had been closed under the Education Act of 1870. With few children available for training, the impetus which led to some better-quality work at the turn of the century soon died. Although lace continued to be made until the First World War, little has been made professionally since then. Honiton's renewed popularity is as an amateur craft hobby.

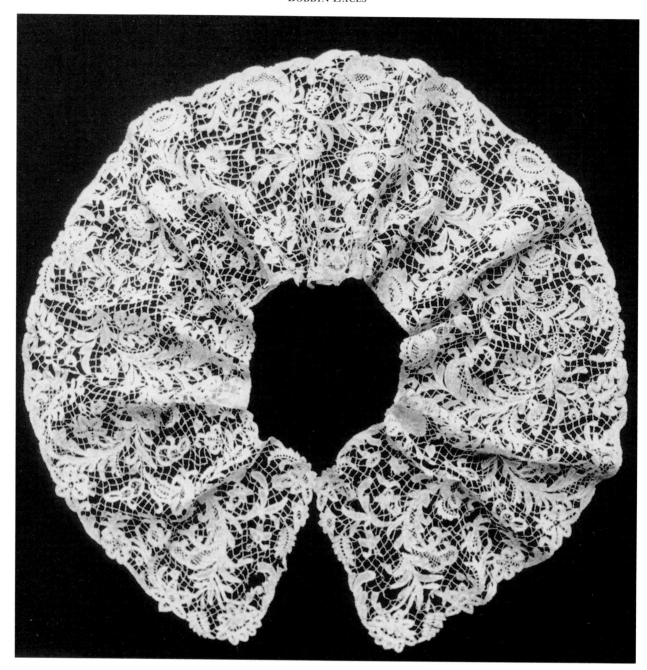

PLATE 116: Bertha collar of Honiton guipure with bobbin-made
brides: about 1850–60.
    Depth of lace 20 cm (8 in)
    Length of inner edge 104 cm (41 in)
This bertha would have been worn around the shoulders of an
evening dress, as seen in Figure 17. It would have needed very little
gathering so that its rich design would have been clearly
displayed. When opened flat it is almost the same shape as the
bertha in Plate 147. Technically the lace is very similar to the
lappet in Plate 117.

PLATE 117: Lappet end of Honiton guipure with bobbin-made brides: about 1850–75.

Maximum width 10 cm (2.5 in)

Length shown 18 cm (7 in)

Full length 96 cm (38 in)

The pair of lappets is made in 19th-century fashion in one continuous length.

The picoted connecting brides are known as 'purl bars' in Honiton lace.

The cabbage roses of this design are almost ubiquitous in Honiton laces; the petals may be made in a continuous spiral as in the central example or in a ring with additional layers worked back and forth as in the outer flowers. The petals are often divided by a gimp thread carried loosely over the surface and alternate petals or layers of petals are commonly worked in half and whole stitches. The flower centres are normally open but for a leadwork filling as in these examples.

Note the raised wings of the butterfly which are attached to the lace only along their inner edges.

a

b

d   c   d

PLATE 118: Group of Honiton laces with different grounds.

a.   Collar with an Alençon-type needlepoint ground (see Plate 119): late 19th century.
     Depth of lace at centre 8 cm (3.2 in)
     Length of inner edge 99 cm (39 in)
The collar has a repeated vine leaf design around the outer edge and a cabbage rose and leaf design around the inner edge but between them is a scattering of unconnected motifs, including birds and butterflies. This lack of order is far more typical of Honiton laces than the organized design of the bertha in Plate 116.

b.   Cuff of Honiton lace with a knotted needlepoint ground (see Plate 119): about 1855–70.
     Depth of lace 7.5 cm (3 in)
This cuff would probably have been worn under a flared outer sleeve of a dress of the late 1850s or 1860s.

c.   Modesty piece of Honiton lace with a needlepoint ground inset in machine-made net: about 1910–30.
     Triangle side 17 cm (6.5 in)
Modesty pieces were used to fill in low-cut necklines; they were particularly common in the 1910s–20s when necklines fell after the very high style of the 1890s–1900s.
     The tape-like design around the central flower sprig is commonly known as 'slugs and snails'.

d.   Pair of mittens of Honiton appliqué on machine-made net with cream silk-satin ribbon trim: late 19th–20th century.
     Length 15 cm (6 in)
The mittens are designed to cover only the palm and base of the thumb and were probably made for a wedding.

PLATE 119:
Above – detail of the cuff in Plate 118*b*.
Below – detail of the collar in Plate 118*a*.

SEVENTEENTH-CENTURY BOBBIN LACES IN THE FLEMISH STYLE, INCLUDING POTTEN KANT LACES

Note and characteristics

This chapter deals with those Flemish laces not considered on pages 92–103. Early 17th century examples are flat laces, made with uniform threads but in any bobbin technique. Later examples are straight laces. 'Potten kants' are characterized by their stylized design of a pot of flowers: they are straight laces, often with a gimp thread and with various mesh grounds.

History

The early development of bobbin laces in the geometric style has already been discussed (pages 82–5) and we have also seen the introduction of floral motifs into needlepoints and into Milanese bobbin laces by the early 17th century. Naturally such changes also occurred in Flemish bobbin laces but here the Flemish manufacturers developed styles which appealed directly to the northern market and were followed in other parts of northern Europe.

The new trend appears to have started with the scalloped edgings of about 1620. The earlier and contemporary geometric laces tended to be very fine and spidery and at first

a

b

c

d

FIGURE 19: Woman's dress of about 1660–70.
By the mid-17th century women's dresses were cut straight at the neckline and were often decorated with a deep fall of lace with a straight or very slightly scalloped edge. A deeper collar was sometimes made up from two flounces, either joined edge to edge, or overlapped, while the neckline might be filled in for modesty as in earlier periods.

PLATE 120:

a. Scallop from a flounce: about 1630–40.
    Maximum depth 11.5 cm (4.5 in)
    Width 9.5 cm (3.7 in)
The broad areas of clothwork, with little relief in the way of filling stitches, are typical of North European laces of the 1630s. The poor delineation of the stylized floral design may be due in part to the technical difficulties found in working more complex designs at this date. There is also a possibility that this lace is English rather than Flemish. It is worked by the part technique.

From the collection of Mrs Valerie Cliffe

b. Flemish edging: about 1740–50.
    Maximum depth 3 cm (1.2 in)
    Pattern repeat 5 cm (2 in)
This is worked by the straight lace technique. The footing and picoted heading are integral.

From the collection of Mrs Kathleen Tipping

c. Flemish edging: about 1740–50.
    Maximum depth 4.5 cm (1.7 in)
    Pattern repeat 5.5 cm (2.5 in)
This is worked by the part technique. The footing and the picoted heading are later additions. The picots are replacements for the original ones which have worn away.

   In addition to the design and workmanship, the extremely fine thread used in this example and in examples (*b*) and (*d*) indicate their Flemish origin: no other country in Europe grew the high-quality flax needed to produce it, nor had the workforce skilled enough to spin it.

d. Flemish edging: about 1760–80.
    Depth 6 cm (2.5 in)
    Pattern repeat 17.5 cm (7 in)
This is worked by the straight lace technique with a kat stitch ground (page 181).

   The repeated cloud-shaped motifs set off against a mesh ground and alternating with symmetrical floral motifs are typical of one branch of Flemish design reputedly made near Antwerp for sale in the Low Countries. This and edging (*a*) in Plate 121 have often been called 'Dutch' laces for this reason.

   An example in the Rougement House Museum, Exeter (Catalogue NO. P327–Palliser Collection) has a design of a double-headed eagle picked out by holes in the clothwork instead of the stylized floral motif seen here. The double-headed eagle was the badge of the Hapsburgs who ruled part of the Netherlands at the time.

From the collection of Mrs Kathleen Tipping

the floral designs were also depicted by narrow bands of clothwork; these were much flatter, softer and more supple than the Milanese bobbin tapes (Plate 78). Some of the areas of clothwork soon broadened out and by the 1630s the deep scallops were filled with an intricate pattern of stylized flowerheads and leaves, sometimes still linked by, or interspersed with, narrow trails of clothwork. The overall arrangement was, of course, one of symmetry about the axis of the scallop as in all other laces of the period. By the 1640s, the scallops were shallower and the pattern had again broken into spidery lines, but now these were closely spaced and separated only by more open lines crossed by a multitude of threads. The basic floral motif is often scarcely discernible in the resulting dense patterning.

   The paucity of remaining examples of mid-17th century Flemish lace makes it difficult to follow subsequent changes but the dense patterning appears to have continued into the 1650s and 1660s as the edge of the lace gradually became straighter. The baroque influence is also seen in the introduction of curving stems but the underlying preference for symmetry is retained as the flounces are divided into panels filled with repeated symmetrical motifs.

   One feature of the later Flemish laces which may, in part, be attributable to these dense designs is the mesh ground. Examples (*b*) and (*c*) in Plate 120, show that these designs were created in both part and straight laces and it is in the latter, in particular, that the primitive mesh is seen. Here, in order to form and, at the same time, to bridge the open areas

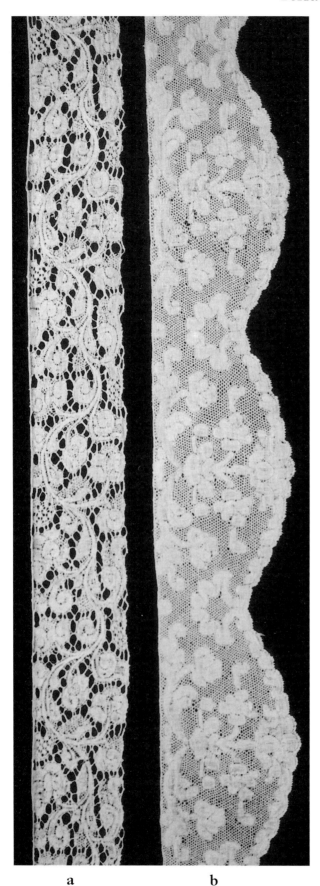

a   b

between the pattern motifs, the threads are plaited and twisted together around irregular voids. The creation of this complex patterning must have taxed the ingenuity of workers in the 1640s to its utmost.

A further example of these early meshes is seen in the baroque lace of Plate 121a. This is again a straight lace despite its flowing design which would be easier to execute by the part technique. It is interesting to compare this lace with the almost contemporary Flemish part laces in Plate 82 and Plate 85a: they all have the same curving stems and spiralling leaves and, although the use of filling stitches is slightly different, a few of the stitches themselves are identical.

By the 1650s or 1660s more regular mesh grounds had also developed as seen in the edgings (d) in Plate 120 and (b) in Plate 121. Both of these laces display a continuation of the symmetrical, floral designs which filled the scallops of the 1630s and the 'Potten kant' laces of the 18th and 19th centuries (Plate 122); this is one of the few laces named for its design rather than its place of origin. The reason for this name, meaning 'pot, or vase, lace' is clear from the vases of flowers depicted.

The 'Potten kants' were marketed particularly in the Netherlands and they show the remarkable strength which tradition can have in a community. Although the design developed in the mid-17th century, and its treatment changed gradually over the centuries, it survived, still recognizable, into the late 19th century.

PLATE 121:
a. Flemish edging: about 1670–90.
   Depth 7 cm (2.7 in)
   Pattern repeat 15 cm (5.7 in)
The design is a peculiarly Flemish version of the Italian baroque style. It is worked as a straight lace with plaited connecting brides (many are repaired).
   This type of design was introduced in the mid-17th century but the scale of the motifs in this example and a loss of boldness in the design suggest the later date. An even later version is seen in the edging added to the Milanese flounce in Plate 75.

b. Flemish edging: about 1660–90.
   Maximum depth 11 cm (4 in)
   Pattern repeat 20.5 cm (8 in)
This is worked as a straight lace with a round Flemish ground, but the ground is worked tightly in the manner of the 18th-century straight Valenciennes laces rather than loosely in the manner of the 17th- and 18th-century part laces.
   Although the scalloped edge of this piece might suggest a date in the 1640s, the open nature of the design indicates the rather later date.

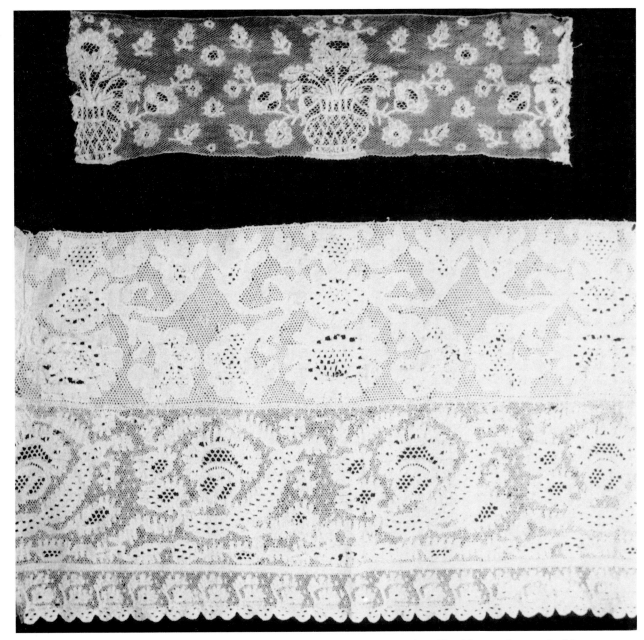

PLATE 122:

a. Flemish potten kant: late 18th–early 19th century.
    Depth 9.5 cm (3.7 in)
    Pattern repeat 16 cm (6.3 in)
This is worked as a straight lace with the Mechlin ground and typical soft Mechlin gimp thread (page 145). The fineness of the thread used, the openness of the design and the scattering of subsidiary motifs are typical of laces of the 1760s to 1780s, but the traditional nature of the potten kant design means that it could be of substantially later date.

Many potten kant laces of the 19th century were worked with the Lille ground (page 151).

b. Upper insertion – Flemish potten kant: early 18th century.
    Depth 11 cm (4.5 in)
    Pattern repeat 17 cm (6.7 in)
This is worked as a straight lace with the round Flemish ground.

The clumsiness of the pattern shows that this was a peasant lace: the care and density of the working and use of the round Flemish ground proclaim it to be earlier than of 19th-century date.

Central insertion: Lille bobbin lace: mid-19th century; about 1830–50.
    Depth 10.5 cm (4 in)
    Pattern repeat 12.5 cm (5 in)
This insertion is of the type known on the continent as 'Lille' (pages 150–3) but it may have been made in northern France or in Belgium. Here it is combined with the earlier potten kant and a narrower edging to form a cap (incomplete).

Lower edging: Lille bobbin lace; mid-19th century; about 1830–50.
    Depth 3.5 cm (1.4 in)
    Pattern repeat 2 cm (0.8 in)

VALENCIENNES

a   b   c

Characteristics

1. Straight bobbin lace.
2. Fine, uniform threads – no raised or gimp outline.
3. Pattern of closely woven clothwork.
4. Rows of generally rectangular holes outline the pattern and separate features within it.
5. Little use of fancy fillings or grounds after the early 18th century.
6. Cut ends of thread at one or each end of pattern motifs in some late 18th century and in most later examples. This is due to additional threads used to increase the density of the clothwork.
7. Grounds:

    a. Round Flemish ground (Figure 20). A hexagonal mesh with four threads plaited or twisted on all six sides enclosing an almost round hole – most common in the mid- to late 18th century.

    b. Diamond ground (Figure 21). Diamond-shaped mesh with four plaited sides – most common in the 19th century.

    c. Snowy (point de neige) ground of complex arrays of interconnected dots common in the early 18th century. Other complex grounds also used in the 18th century.

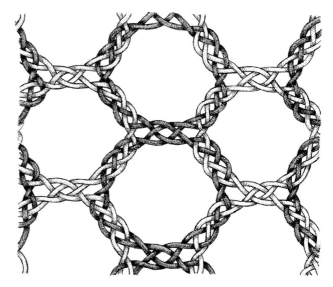

FIGURE 20: The Valenciennes round ground.

PLATE 123: **Group of lappets.**

a. (*centre*). About 1720–30.
   Length shown 39 cm (15 in)
   Full length 63 cm (25 in)
A later form of the 'bizarre' patterns is shown here; the design is less crowded than those of the late 1710s–early 20s but the motifs are still richly patterned with filling stitches and geometric shapes and there is strong movement from side to side. The ground is a 'five-hole' ground.

b. (*right*). About 1765–80. (See Plate 125 for detail.)
   Length shown 33 cm (13 in)
   Full length 67 cm (26.5 in)
Here is the classic form of Valenciennes lace: the design is in dense clothwork with internal features picked out by rows of holes; the ground is the round Flemish ground and no filling stitches are used.

c. (*left*). About 1780–90.
   Length shown 33 cm (13 in)
   Full length 55 cm (22 in)
Note the lightness of the mesh ground compared with that of the right-hand lappet in this plate: this results from the use of the diamond ground instead of the round ground. The density of the clothwork is enhanced by the introduction of a few extra threads which do not continue into the ground but are cut off at the upper edges of the motifs: this shows that the lappet was started at the rounded end.

FIGURE 21: The Valenciennes diamond ground.

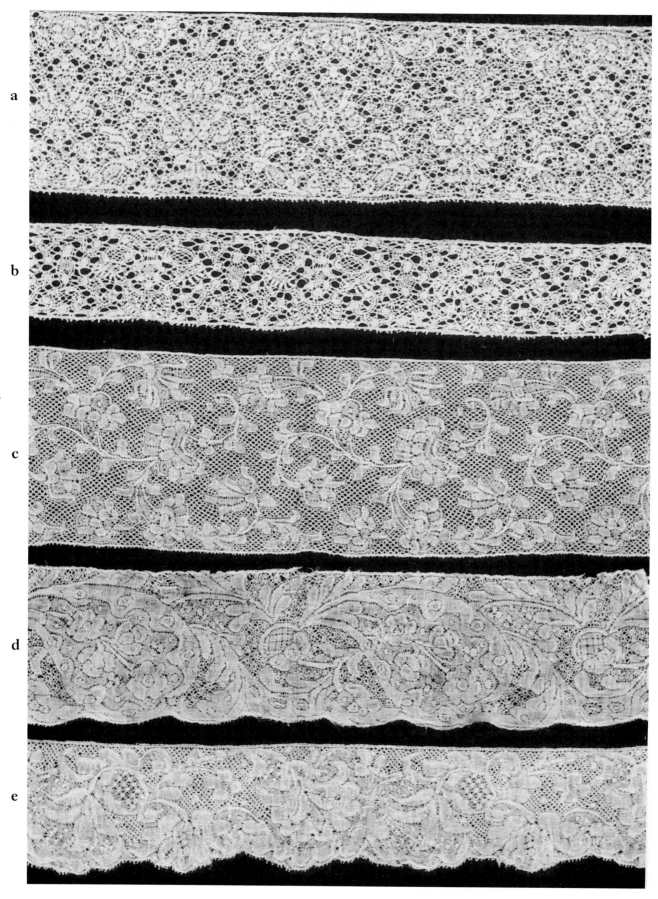

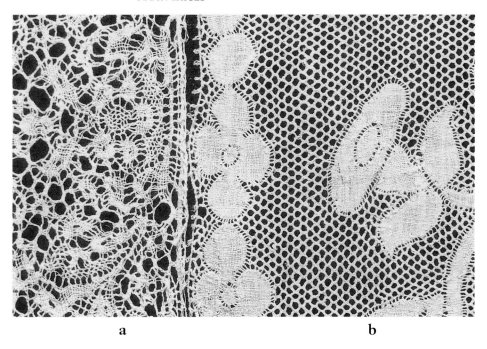

a   b

PLATE 124: A group of Valenciennes edgings: length shown 21.5 cm (8.5 in).

a.   About 1700; 1695–1710.
     Depth 6.5 cm (2.6 in)
     Pattern repeat 9.5 cm (3.8 in)
The design, although confused, is essentially a 'candelabra' pattern (see Plate 90*a*). The ground is a very open, irregular form of the snowy ground used in example (*d*) below. This, and edging (*b*), below, are of a type previously ascribed to Binche.

b.   About 1700.
     Depth 3.5 cm (1.4 in)
     Pattern repeat 6 cm (2.4 in)
Note the use of half stitch and tallies.

c.   About 1700–20.
     Depth 7 cm (2.8 in)
     Pattern repeat 9 cm (3.6 in)
This light design of separate, curving, asymmetric sprigs is quite common in Valenciennes laces and appears to date from the early 18th century.

d.   About 1715–25.
     Depth 5.5 cm (2.2 in)
     Pattern repeat 11 cm (4.4 in)
Bizarre style with a snowy ground.

e.   About 1725–40.
     Depth 4.5 cm (1.8 in)
     Pattern repeat 11.5 cm (4.6 in)
Five-hole ground with snowy ground as a filling.

Points to watch

The only constant factors in Valenciennes lace are the very fine thread used and the total lack of thick outlining which makes it completely flat.

The 'snowy' ground which was common in the early 18th century was long thought to have originated in Binche, a Flemish town about 50 km (30 miles) from Valenciennes, but there are no clear records of this town's products in the early 18th century. By the mid-18th century, Binche was certainly making straight laces similar to those of Valenciennes but so were many other lace-making towns and Binche was also making motifs for Brussels part laces. There is thus insufficient evidence for us to identify flat laces with a snowy ground as a distinct type and to ascribe them to Binche.

Very close copies of Valenciennes laces were made by machine in the 19th century.

History

It is rare that history relates the names of those involved in the lace trade but records indicate that the first important manufacturer in Valenciennes was one Françoise Badar. She herself was a lace-maker, having learnt the craft in Antwerp, and she taught the Valenciennes people to make both bobbin and needle laces. In the late 1640s and 1650s, the industry grew under her direction and she was soon joined by other manufacturers.

This early prosperity was not to last. In the wars between France and Spain for dominion over the Low Countries, Valenciennes became a battlefield and the settlement of 1678, which ceded Valenciennes to France, brought little relief. The heavy taxes imposed on Valenciennes' products made them uncompetitive and it was not until the 1720s that

FIGURE 22: By the mid-18th century, men had ceased to wear cravats with elaborate lace ends (see Figure 14, page 101) except on formal occasions. The lace seen in portraits of the second half of the century consists of the shirt ruffles: these include edgings gathered down the front opening which project between the edges of the waistcoat and matching edgings which fall over the wrists. By the early 19th century even this use had ceased except for formal wear.

PLATE 126: A group of Valenciennes edgings.

a. About 1730–40.
    Depth 5.5 cm (2.2 in)
    Pattern repeat 11.5 cm (4.5 in)

b. About 1730–50.
    Depth 2.5 cm (1 in)
    Pattern repeat 13.5 cm (5.3 in)

c. About 1740–55.
    Depth 3.5 cm (1.4 in)
    Pattern repeat 13 cm (5.2 in)

d. About 1755–70.
    Depth 4.5 cm (1.8 in)
    Pattern repeat 19 cm (7.5 in)
The drawing of this edging is not so fine as that of edgings (a) to (c) and (e) and it is worked in a coarser thread. It would have sold to the lower end of the market. It uses the 5-hole ground.

e. About 1765–80.
    Depth 5 cm (2 in)
    Pattern repeat 12 cm (4.8 in)

f. About 1780–1800.
    Depth 6 cm (2.4 in)
    Pattern repeat 10 cm (4 in)

fashion and the economic climate again turned in Valenciennes' favour.

In the intervening years, changes had occurred within the Flemish industry and the products of various of the lace-making towns had diverged. Whereas Brussels had become known for her fine-quality part laces, Valenciennes' workers had specialized in a straight lace. This in turn was differentiated from straight laces of the Antwerp area by the introduction of new French designs. These at first followed the Bérainesque style but it was the introduction and development of the 'bizarre' designs which coincided with, and perhaps brought about, the revival of the industry.

A further major contribution to the advances of the lace industry in this period was the refinement of the thread manufacture. Flanders had long been renowned for the quality of her linen but now her workforce was able to produce thread only a few fibres thick and with a count which has been estimated at about 1200 (the finest linen thread now available is far coarser, with a count of about 320). It was this thread which was used in many of the exquisite edgings and lappets of the early 18th century which required up to 800 bobbins to create a width of only 10 cm (4 in).

Throughout the middle decades of the 18th century, Valenciennes was in great demand with the aristocracy who prized it not only for the delicacy and beauty of its designs but also for the strength and firmness of its structure which made it very durable even through repeated washings. The success of the Valenciennes industry naturally led to copying in other lace-making centres but it was always said that the refinement of true Valenciennes lace distinguished it from imitations, or 'fausses Valenciennes'. Certainly, at the time, the industry within the city was highly organized and great care was taken over the quality of thread used, over consistency of workmanship and over design but we can rarely be certain of the origin of surviving examples.

In the later 18th century, as fashion turned to lighter fabrics, Valenciennes' popularity waned but efforts were made to compete. Additional threads were introduced into the clothwork to increase the contrast between the pattern and the ground which could thus be made more open and, in some cases, the lighter diamond-shaped mesh was used. These could not, however, halt the decline and the French revolution effectively brought lace-making in the town itself to an end.

In the 19th century, the Valenciennes tradition was continued in other centres, but particularly in Belgium. The diamond-shaped mesh became more firmly established and its scale increased to heighten the contrast with the pattern and to quicken production. The extra threads which had at first been added into the clothwork at the beginning of each new pattern area and taken out at the end, leaving cut ends at one edge, were now carried loosely over the back of the ground from one motif to the next. When the lace was finished they were then cut at both ends of the motif.

PLATE 127: Group of 19th–20th C edgings. Length shown 20 cm (8 in).

a. About 1800–10.
    Depth 7.5 cm (2.9 in)
    Pattern repeat 2 cm (0.7 in)

b. Mid-late 19th C.
    Depth 6.5 cm (2.6 in)
    Pattern repeat 7 cm (2.8 in)
Although the pattern of this piece probably dates from about the 1840s, it is worked in a fairly heavy thread, probably for the peasant market, and could be of a much later date. The ground is a rather open version of the round Flemish ground which is associated with 19th-century Valenciennes laces made in Dieppe.

c. Late 19th C; probably about 1855–75.
    Depth 10 cm (4 in)
    Pattern repeat 6.5 cm (2.6 in)

d. Late 19th–early 20th C.
    Maximum depth 4.5 cm (1.8 in)
    Pattern repeat 2 cm (1.9 in)
This is yet another example of a late 19th–20th century lace copying an early style. Here the dentate edge common in early 19th-century edgings is mixed with a repeated sprig motif also used at that time, but the larger scale of the design and the thread used indicate the later date.

Despite these changes, Valenciennes was still a slow and difficult lace to make and much of its production in the nineteenth century was in the form of narrow trimmings and insertions. Compared with other laces it was always expensive but its smoothness and strength made it particularly suitable for underwear and babies' wear and there was always a ready market.

In the lace boom of the 1850s and 1860s some manufacturers were able to increase their range of Valenciennes laces, even to the extent of producing wide flounces. Shading was introduced by the contrasting use of whole and half stitch, as it was in other laces of this period, and the better manufacturers even took to dividing more elaborate designs into sections for working by the part technique. This type of lace came to be known as 'Valenciennes de Gand', after Gand (or Ghent) the home of the more influential manufacturers who made these products.

As with other hand-lace industries, the manufacture of Valenciennes lace could not survive long after 1900 but the interest in antique laces at the turn of the century brought a curious revival. This was the return of laces with the complex snowy ground and sprinklings of points d'esprit. These are still made commercially to a limited extent and now sell under the name of 'point de fée'.

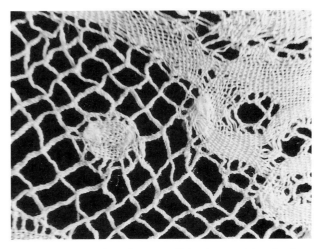

PLATE 128: Detail of a 19th-century Valenciennes edging showing the diamond-mesh ground and cut ends of thread at each end of the clothwork where extra threads, added to increase its density, have been cut away.

PLATE 129:
a.   Edging: about 1870–1900.
     Depth 6.5 cm (2.6 in)
     Pattern repeat 8 cm (3.2 in)
In the later 19th century, half stitch was introduced into the pattern to give a more naturalistic effect as it was in many other laces of the period.

MECHLIN

(MALINES/MECHELEN)

PLATE 130: Cap back: 1735–45.
    Width 8 cm (3.1 in)
    Depth 9 cm (3.5 in)
This is clearly made in two panels; the technique of joining panels
invisibly by the point de racroc had not yet been invented. The
cartouches of fancy filling stitches are particularly characteristic
of mid-18th-century Mechlin laces.
    The cap back formed the centre of a woman's formal head-
dress: a gathered edging sewn around the curved edge would have
formed a frill framing the face while a pair of lappets would have
hung from the sides or from the straight edge at the back (see
Figure 6, page 40).

Characteristics

1. Straight bobbin lace in fine, soft, white thread.
2. Clothwork pattern.
3. Gimp thread outline to the pattern. The gimp is usually slight, soft and silky but a heavy thread was sometimes used in the 18th century.
4. Frequent use of cartouches and other areas filled with fancy stitches.
5. Ground (see Figure 23):
    Hexagonal mesh with two sides of four plaited threads and four sides of two threads twisted or crossed.

Points to watch

The Mechlin ground is very similar to the Brussels vrai drochel (Figure 15, page 105) but the Mechlin plaits are shorter by one half stitch giving the mesh the appearance of a regular hexagon.

History

Mechlin (Malines in French) is a small Flemish town to the north of Brussels and not far from Antwerp. As early as the 16th century it was a centre of the lace-making industry and by the late 17th century its name was probably in use as a generic term for Flemish straight laces.

In the early 18th century, as laces from the various towns acquired the distinct characteristics now associated with them, Mechlin became known for its straight lace made in a fine, soft, white thread. It was this, as much as the gimp introduced in this period, that distinguished Mechlin lace from that of Brussels and Valenciennes which were worked in a more tightly twisted, creamy thread.

In other respects there was little difference between the early products of Mechlin and Valenciennes: they were both worked in the intricate designs of the period and with a variety of complex meshes. Not until the 1740s did the fine hexagonal mesh we associate with Mechlin laces become firmly established but this was retained for the rest of its history save always, of course, for the occasional exception.

From its early period, Mechlin retained one other feature: the use of complex fillings often arranged in the odd cartouche shapes of the bizarre period. These are seen in their most accomplished form in the cap back and lappet of Plates 130 and 132 and continued well into the second half of the century.

Throughout this early period Mechlin was widely regarded as the 'Queen of Laces' and was particularly popular in England. Its soft texture had suited the styles even of the 1700s but, by the 1760s and 1770s, the crisper texture of needlepoint was again in fashion. It is probable that the thicker, corded gimp was introduced into some Mechlin laces at this period in imitation of the stiff cordonnet of the French needlepoints: an example is seen in Plate 134a.

It was also at this period that Mechlin came to be regarded as a 'summer' lace by the French court; it suited the softer, lighter fabrics worn in the summer months whereas French

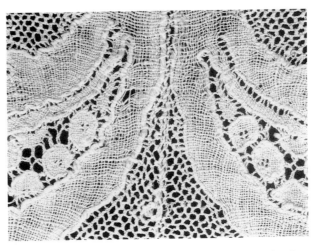

PLATE 131: Detail of Plate 130 showing the Mechlin ground and untwisted gimp outline to the pattern.

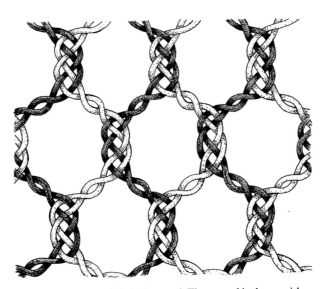

FIGURE 23: The Mechlin 'eis' ground. The ground is shown with twisted threads on four sides, but these threads are often simply crossed, particularly in 18th century laces.

The ground is shown with twisted threads on four sides, but these threads are often simply crossed, particularly in 18th century laces.

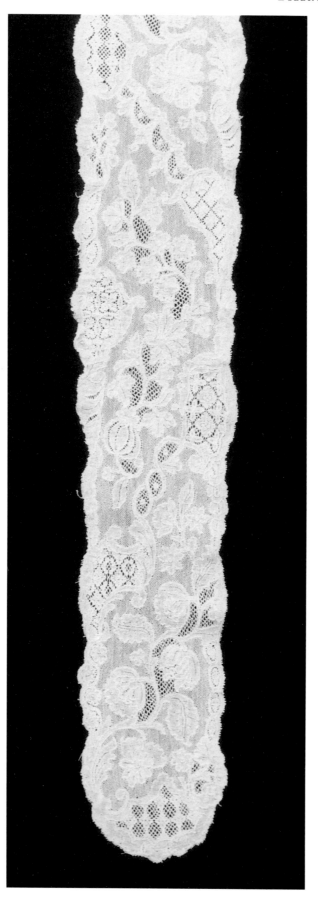

needlepoints were *de rigueur* in the winter. No doubt this usage, together with its popularity in Britain, enabled its production to continue, if on a reduced scale, through the slump at the end of the century.

Naturally by this time its designs had changed. The rich patterns of earlier decades were replaced by simple, repeated classical motifs and flowerheads. In these there was little room for Mechlin's accustomed virtuosity of filling stitches.

The early 19th century brought continued change in design as it did in other laces but the Mechlin technique could not cope successfully with the larger fashion accessories required in the second half of the century. Being a straight lace, it could not, like the Brussels laces, make use of machine nets to quicken production. Nor was it strong enough for the accustomed uses of Valenciennes lace.

It remained a slow and laborious lace to make, and commensurately expensive. Although its production continued in the later nineteenth century and occasionally wide flounces were made, it never regained its former importance and little has been made this century.

PLATE 132: Lappet: 1735–45.
Length shown 51 cm (20 in)
Full length 58 cm (23 in)

a

b

c

d

PLATE 133: Group of Mechlin edgings: length shown 27.5 cm (11 in).

a. About 1720–40.
    Depth 4.5 cm (1.8 in)
    Pattern repeat 16.5 cm (6.5 in)
The footing is 18th century and may even be the original one.

b. About 1730–50.
    Depth 4 cm (1.6 in)
    Pattern repeat 18 cm (7 in)
The footing is of much later date. A complex ground is used here
but the gimp thread and use of fillings in the design are typical of
Mechlin laces.

c. About 1745–60.
    Depth 4.5 cm (1.8 in)
    Pattern repeat 21 cm (8.3 in)
Many mid-18th-century edgings were worked in designs which
could be sewn edge-to-edge, as shown here, to form a double frill
with the pattern continuing across the join.

d. About 1755–70.
    Depth 3.5 cm (1.4 in)
    Pattern repeat 16 cm (6.3 in)
A complex ground is again used and the footing is again of later
date.

PLATE 134: **Late 18th C edgings: length shown 27 cm (10.5 in).**

a. About 1755–75.
   Depth 4.5 cm (1.8 in)
   Pattern repeat 18 cm (7 in)
The extremely thick corded gimp thread used here stands proud
on the right side of the lace, in imitation of the raised work of
French needlepoints which were particularly fashionable at the
time.

b. About 1765–80.
   Depth 5 cm (2 in)
   Pattern repeat 18.5 cm (7.3 in)

c. About 1770–85.
   Depth 5 cm (2 in)
   Pattern repeat 17 cm (6.7 in)

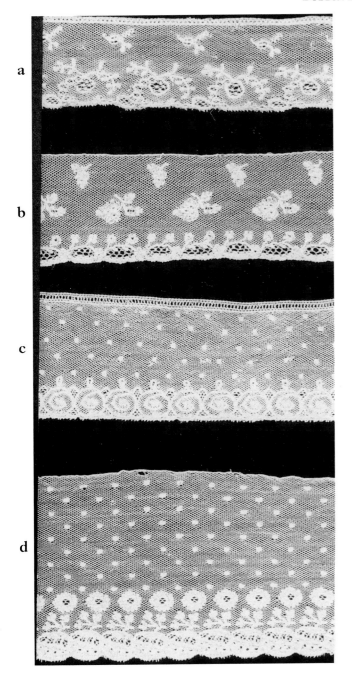

PLATE 135: Late 18th C–early 19th C edgings: length shown 14 cm (5.5 in).

a. About 1775–1800.
  Depth 4 cm (1.6 in)
  Pattern repeat 4 cm (1.6 in)

b. About 1775–1800.
  Depth 5 cm (2 in)
  Pattern repeat 3.5 cm (1.9 in)

c. About 1800–1810.
  Depth 6 cm (2.5 in)
  Pattern repeat 1.5 cm (0.6 in)

d. About 1810–1820.
  Depth 9 cm (8.5 in)
  Pattern repeat 2 cm (0.8 in)

PLATE 136: 19th C edgings: length shown 15 cm (6 in).

a. About 1820–30.
  Depth 8.5 cm (3.9 in)
  Pattern repeat 4 cm (1.6 in)

b. About 1830–45.
  Depth 5.5 cm (2.2 in)
  Pattern repeat 5 cm (2 in)

c. About 1850–75.
  Depth 6.5 cm (2.6 in)
  Pattern repeat 7 cm (2.8 in)

d. About 1890–1910.
  Depth 6 cm (2.4 in)
  Pattern repeat 3 cm (1.2 in)

LILLE

PLATE 137: Veil or apron: probably Lille: about 1800.
  Depth shown 38 cm (15 in)
  Full depth (*centre*) 73 cm (29 in); ends 98 cm (34 in)
  Pattern repeat 21.5 cm (8.5 in)
  Full width 135 cm (53 in)
18th-century aprons are typically deeper at the ends than in the
centre which suggests that this piece may be an apron but the
difference may be due simply to uneven stretching from wear and
washing. The pattern is sliced through at the ends rather than
being arranged with side borders: the top edge is turned over to
take a draw string.
  In the late 18th and early 19th centuries most lace was made in
the form of narrow edgings patterned with repeated flowerheads
or tenuous, classical motifs along the headside; but the occasional
larger articles often had classical designs such as this. The spikey
nature of the sprigs suggests a Lille origin although similar work
was carried out in England.

Characteristics

1. Straight bobbin lace.
2. Gimp thread outline to the pattern.
3. Clothwork pattern frequently including narrow and/or branching lines.
4. Few filling stitches used but often of large scale leaving relatively large openings.
5. Ground (Figure 24):
   Fond simple (known in the UK as East Midlands or Buckinghamshire point ground). Hexagonal mesh with four sides of two twisted threads and two sides of two threads crossed. Laces with this ground date from the late 18th century to the present day.

Points to watch

The fond simple ground may well have originated in Lille but was in use throughout Europe in the 19th century. Laces technically of Lille type came to be known by local names, such as Buckinghamshire point (see pages 154–61) and are often indistinguishable from each other unless design characteristics link them to a particular country of origin.

PLATE 138: **Detail of Plate 137.**

FIGURE 24: **Fond simple or Lille ground.**

History

Lille, like Valenciennes, was a Flemish lace-making town ceded to France in the late 17th century. Its workers continued to make lace in the Flemish tradition and in the early 18th century made inferior copies of the Mechlin and Valenciennes laces.

Their other major product was a poorer-quality linen lace for the peasant markets which was worked in simple, often geometric patterns against a variety of light, open grounds. In the 1760s and 1770s this became fashionable and, as dress continued to simplify with the introduction of neo-classical styles, the market for lightly-patterned trimmings grew.

During this period an even lighter net developed. This was the fond simple, a simple twist net which, along with the straggly, branching designs of the period, we have come to associate with Lille lace.

Over the next 40 years the Lille industry did not suffer as greatly as other parts of the French lace industry but it did see a succession of declines and resurgences as it competed against revolution, war and the growing market in machine-made nets. By the 1830s it was again flourishing and the neo-

classical design had given way to patterns of floral sprigs. The subsequent changes to richer, more elaborate patterns were not so successful. This essentially lightweight lace could no longer compete with the luxurious needlepoints and heavier bobbin laces of Brussels. The development of the machine industry was a final blow. This had copied the Lille ground from an early date and the attachment of the Jacquard device to the lace machines in the 1840s enabled the net to be patterned at will.

Although lace continued to be made in northern France and Belgium by the Lille technique in the later 19th century, much of the produce was again for the peasant market. Design became stereotyped, workmanship deteriorated and the quantity produced gradually fell away.

PLATE 139:
a. Edging: about 1775–1790.
    Depth 4.5 cm (1.7 in)
    Pattern repeat 4 cm (1.5 in)
This edging could have been made in Lille or in the English East Midlands.

b. Lille edging: about 1780–1800.
    Depth 10 cm (4 in)
    Pattern repeat 7 cm (2.8 in)
Branching designs formed by extremely narrow areas of clothwork bounded by gimp thread, with minor areas of very open filling stitches, are thought to be particularly characteristic of Lille work.

c. Lille edging: mid-19th C.
    Depth 9 cm (3.5 in)
    Pattern repeat 6 cm (2.4 in)
The thread used in this 19th-century example is much coarser than that of the 18th-century examples and the net ground has larger meshes. It was thus quicker to work, cheaper and more suited to compete with machine products. It is worked without a footing and was probably intended to be joined along the footside to an insertion strip to make a wider flounce. Interestingly, some of the clothwork is worked in the ground thread and some in the gimp to give different densities.

PLATE 140: Bonnet veil: about 1850–60.
    Depth shown 40.5 cm (16 in)
    Full depth of veil 48 cm (19 in)
    Length shown 58 cm (23 in)
    Full length of veil 114 cm (45 in)
The top edge is finished with a footing. The strips from which this veil is made are clearly visible; the floral band above the scalloped edge is of much higher quality than the sprigged ground above it while the edge itself is of intermediate quality. The organization of the design within the scalloped border, the beautiful drawing of the flowers, and their naturalistic rendering with the use of half stitch together with the cloth stitch to give the effect of shading all combine to suggest a French origin: indeed, a similar treatment of the flowers can be seen in some designs from Caen, but it has been suggested by a highly reputable expert that this piece might be English.

EAST MIDLANDS
(BUCKINGHAMSHIRE) POINT

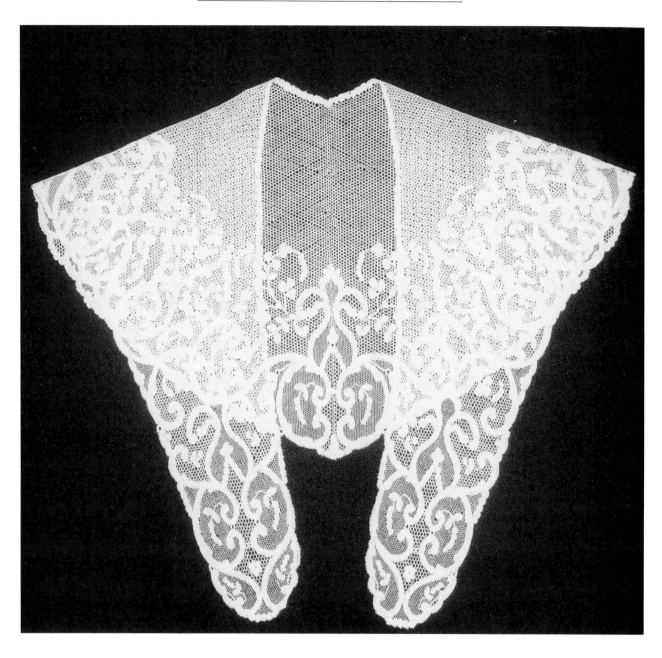

PLATE 141: Shawl collar: about 1835–45.
   Depth at centre 28.5 cm (11 in)
The design shows the mixture of influences that were current in
the late 1830s–40s. The major area of the ground is worked in kat
stitch while point ground is used in the stylized edge motifs. (See
Plate 142 for detail.)

Characteristics

1. Straight bobbin lace.
2. Clothwork pattern is most common except in black laces where half stitch is more usual.
3. Gimp thread outline to the pattern.
4. Areas of fancy filling stitches common, particularly honeycomb and honeycomb with mayflowers (small blocks of whole stitch).
5. Grounds:
   a. Point ground (fond simple, see Figure 25). Hexagonal mesh with four sides of two twisted threads and two sides of two threads crossed.
   b. Kat stitch (also known as wire ground, point de Paris, Chantilly ground – fond chant, see Figure 26). Hexagonal mesh giving the appearance of a six-pointed star – the central hole is surrounded by six smaller holes each formed by a triangle of three pairs of threads.

Points to watch

East Midlands lace with the point ground is technically similar to Lille lace (see pages 150–3). Similar laces with the kat stitch ground were also made on the Continent.

Good machine copies of point ground were made in the early 19th century, shortly followed by the kat stitch ground.

Simple needle-run, or darned, machine nets (see pages 76–8) can easily be mistaken for East Midlands bobbin laces.

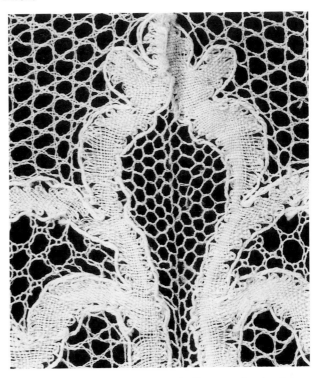

PLATE 142: Detail of the shawl collar in Figure 142 showing the central join between the two halves of the collar, an area of point ground in the centre, the kat stitch ground at the top, and areas of 'honeycomb' filling (*right and left centre*).

FIGURE 25: **East Midlands point ground (fond simple etc.)**

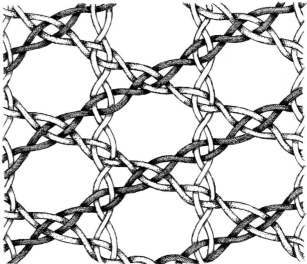

FIGURE 26: **Kat stitch ground.**

History

The tradition of lace-making in the English East Midlands counties of Bedfordshire, Buckinghamshire and Northamptonshire goes back at least to the 17th century but the products of these early years are no longer specifically identifiable and the same is true for much of the 18th-century production. By this time lace in the style of the poorer-quality continental products, with light, open grounds and simple patterns, was being made although the

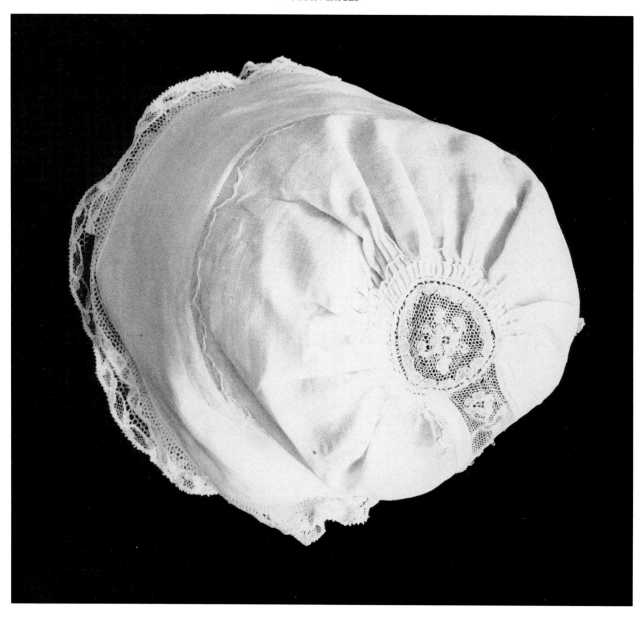

PLATE 143: Baby's bonnet: about 1770–1800.
   Diameter of lace cap back 3 cm (1.3 in)
   Depth of edging 1 cm (0.5 in)
Narrow, lightly patterned edgings and insertions constituted a
major proportion of the East Midlands output in both the 18th and
19th centuries. Many were used as in this example to decorate
babies' wear and were known as 'baby laces'.

Mechlin laces, so beloved of the English aristocracy, were
probably copied as well.

If one studies the portraiture of the 1750s and 1760s one
sees a greater use of these lighter laces. Large accessories,
such as capes and flounces, were made up from strips joined
edge to edge while flowing sleeve ruffles often consisted the
lighter, cheaper product with perhaps an edging of more
expensive lace.

In the 1770s the American War of Independence was as
much a blow to the Midlands industry as it was to Devon.
Lace-making, which had spread to surrounding counties in
the previous years of prosperity, drew back into the major
centres. This was to be a recurring process over the next
hundred years or more as the trade struggled against the
vagaries of fashion and the growth of the machine industry.

In the 1790s and early 1800s, revolution and war were for
once in its favour. With the diminishing flow of lace from the

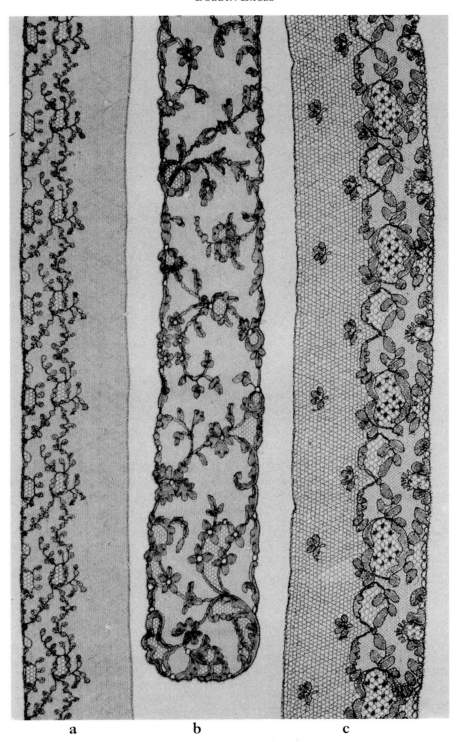

a   b   c

PLATE 144: Group of East Midlands black point laces. These are technically the same as Chantilly laces with their use of half stitch instead of cloth stitch for the pattern. The two edgings are, however, worked in a shiny thread and their designs are typical of English manufacture. The central lappet is in the dull grenadine thread of Chantilly but is still likely to be of English manufacture.

a. (*left*). Edging with the point ground and 'honeycomb' fillings: about 1830–40.
    Depth 9 cm (3.5 in)
    Pattern repeat 7.5 cm (3 in)

b.   One of a pair of lappets made in a single length: about 1840–50.
    Width 9 cm (3.5 in)
    Length shown 53 cm (21 in)
    Full length 112 cm (44 in)

c. (*right*). Edging with the kat stitch ground near the footside and the point ground near the headside and with 'honeycomb' and 'honeycomb-with-mayflower' fillings.
    Depth 12 cm (4.5 in)
    Pattern repeat 11.5 cm (4.5 in)

PLATE 145:

a. Baby's bonnet of East Midlands point lace with a circular back of darned machine net: mid-19th C.

Diameter of cap back 6 cm (2.2 in)

The bonnet is made up from a series of narrow insertions of point lace and a circular cap back of embroidered net. Simple designs such as these continued in use for decades and are impossible to date with any accuracy.

b. Lower part of an East Midlands point flounce: about 1820–30.

Width shown 38 cm (15 in)

Depth shown 29 cm (11.5 in)

Full depth 106 cm (42 in)

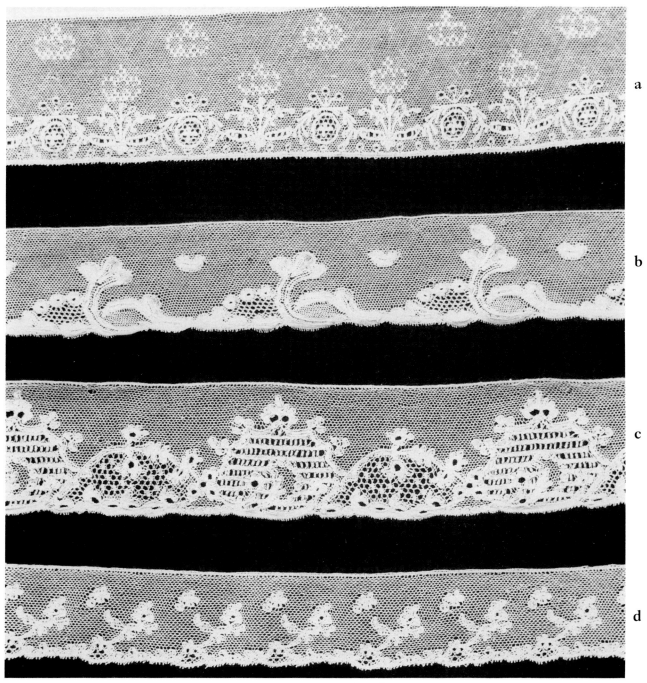

a

b

c

d

PLATE 146: Group of 19th-C point ground edgings: length shown
30 cm (12 in).

a. About 1805–15.
   Depth 7.5 cm (3 in)
   Pattern repeat 6.5 cm (2.6 in)
Note the straight edge, finely drawn classical motifs including a
laurel wreath, and the crowns picked out by tallies in the ground.

b. About 1820–40.
   Depth 5.5 cm (2.1 in)
   Pattern repeat 9.5 cm (3.7 in)
The gimp thread is used within the motifs rather than as an
outlining thread. This form is sometimes called 'Regency point'
but its design indicates that it is of later date than the Regency
period.

c. About 1840–50.
   Depth 6.5 cm (2.6 in)
   Pattern repeat 13 cm (5.1 in)
Designs of odd-shaped cartouches outlined with stylized flowers
and filled with fancy stitches in the mid-18th-century manner are
particularly common in East Midlands laces after about 1840.

d. Post-1850.
   Depth 4 cm (1.6 in)
This is an example of the much simplified designs current in the
later part of the 19th century.

continent and the continuing interest in lighter laces, particularly in wide expanses of net, the East Midlands industry was stimulated to greater production. During the previous decades the lighter Lille ground, known in England as point ground, had been introduced and this was now used to create veils, stoles, shawls or even over-dresses. These, in the style of their time, were sprinkled with spots or tiny motifs and edged with a light pattern of repeated flowerheads or delicately drawn motifs. Usually these were arranged along a straight edge but a pointed edge was also common.

Surviving pieces of Midlands lace enable one to follow the development of design through the early 19th century. The pointed edges of the 1800s to 1810s became gradually more rounded as the simple flowerheads or upright sprigs developed a curving form, then grew in size to fill the broader, scalloped edges of the 1830s. At the same time, flowing linear patterns or repeated examples of the curving sprig motif developed inside, but spaced from the decorative edge. Usually the major proportion of the lace was still composed of spotted net but occasionally narrow, floral designs snaked vertically up the ground. In the 1830s these gradually widened at the bottom until the broad triangular form of the 1840s (see Plate 114) was reached.

Throughout this period the design was expanding gradually up into the net and becoming ever more elaborate. By the 1840s a desire for all-over patterning had returned but the expertise required to draw the necessary designs had long since vanished. Earlier laces, particularly those of the mid-18th century, were looked to for inspiration. The result was a mixture of naturalistic floral designs, often intermingled with light rococo scrolls or ribbonwork, of more stylized designs with cartouches of fancy fillings and occasionally of stylized classical designs.

Unfortunately for the Midlands industry, the competition from machine laces had now reached a climax. The point ground, which was the simplest of the hand-made nets, had been copied by machine at an early stage. In its infancy, both fashion and the novelty of machine-made net had made it desirable and the hand-lace industry had declined but, in the late 1820s and 1830s, the tables were turned as machines could not yet produce the patterned fabrics fashion demanded. For a while the Midlands laces, but more especially the French blondes, could compete in price and popularity with the hand-embroidered nets and muslins and it was the machine-lace industry that suffered.

Enormous efforts were now devoted to the patterning of machine-made net and in the 1840s, the Jacquard machine, which had been developed to quicken the production of brocades, was applied to lace manufacture. Although many developments had yet to come, from this point on, machine-made lace could, effectively, be patterned at will.

By the late 1840s the Midlands point lace could no longer compete in price with machine-made copies. Its light ground and straight technique were not, in any case, suited to produce the heavier, more richly patterned laces that were coming into fashion. Many of its workers turned to making the guipure laces discussed in a later chapter; many others left the industry altogether.

Although its production continued through the second half of the 19th century, the making of larger accessories disappeared. Only the narrow edgings, in simple versions of the earlier designs, remained. The 1890s and early 1900s brought something of a revival but the previous prosperity of the industry was never regained.

PLATE 147:
a. Fall cap: about 1850–60.
    Length 100 cm (40 in)
    Depth at centre 29 cm (12 in)

b. Bertha collar: 1840–60.
    Length of inner edge 79 cm (31.5 in)
    Depth 22.5 cm (9 in)
Tiered berthas made up from several overlapping lace edgings
like this were very popular in the mid-19th century in addition to
berthas made from a complete panel of lace like that in Plate 116.
The design of the lace edging was in use over several decades.

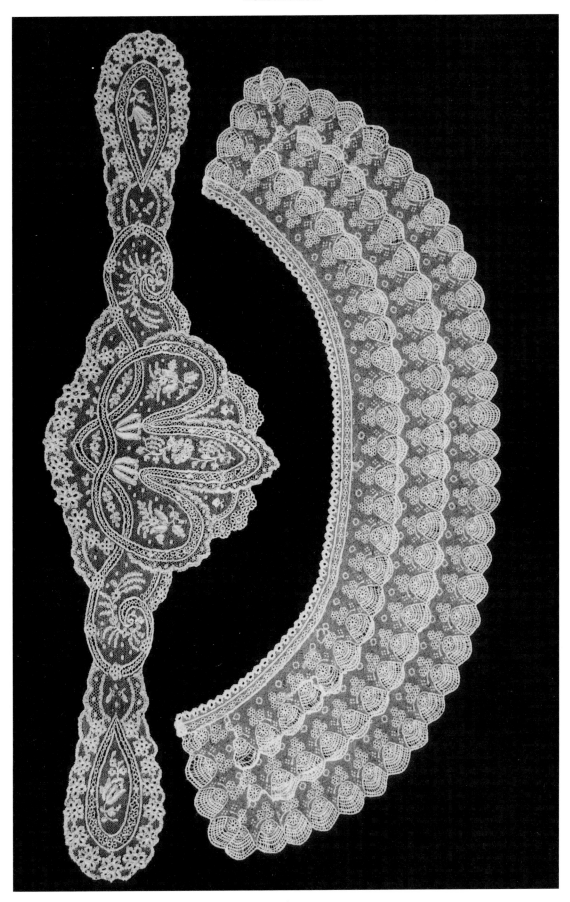

BLONDE

PLATE 148: Double fichu collar of silk blonde lace, probably from
Caen or Bayeux: about 1835–40.
   Maximum width as shown 64 cm (25 in)
Large double collars of this type were extremely popular from the
1820s to the 1840s; the shape varied gradually to suit the shoulder
outline created by the dress underneath. This example has the
typical scalloped edge of the late 1820s to early 1830s, with each
scallop filled with a single flowerhead, but the spread of the leafy
sprigs into the net ground suggests a date in the late 1830s. When
unfolded it does not lie flat; it is definitely shaped to be worn
double and to fit the curve of the shoulders.

Characteristics

1. Straight bobbin lace in silk thread – cream, black or ivory.
2. Dense, shiny pattern areas in thick floss silk set off against a very light ground in a very much finer, twisted thread.
3. Floss silk or corded silk used to outline the pattern or to form linear patterns.
4. Some half-stitch pattern areas in the fine ground thread.
5. Grounds:

   a. Fond simple (East Midlands point ground, Figure 25, page 155). Hexagonal mesh with four sides of two twisted threads and two sides of two threads crossed.

   b. Paris ground (also known as kat stitch etc, Figure 26, page 155). Hexagonal mesh giving the appearance of a six-pointed star – the central hole is surrounded by six smaller holes each formed by a triangle of three pairs of threads.

Points to watch

Close copies of blonde laces were made by darning silk machine nets with a floss silk thread (see Plate 68): in darned work the floss silk is seen passing in and out of the meshes of the net, but in true blonde, the floss silk is trapped between the finer threads of the ground.

I have found a number of larger articles, apparently of blonde lace but with a plain net centre which, on close inspection, I found to be machine net very cunningly joined to a blonde edging.

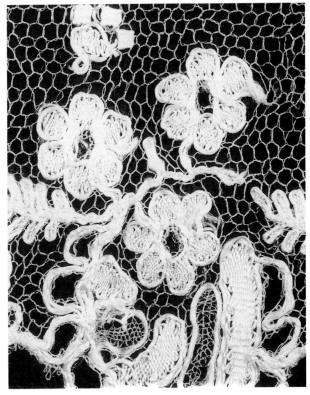

PLATE 149: Detail of Plate 150a showing the contrast between the extremely fine thread used for the ground and the half stitch pattern areas, the floss silk used for the cloth stitch and, in this case, the even thicker gimp thread. The ground, though much worn, is of the simple Lille type.

History

Silk laces were made throughout the 17th and 18th centuries but the perishable nature of the thread has meant that little has survived and we must look to written records and to portraiture for their history. The type known as 'blonde', from its natural, creamy colour, became popular in the 1750s when it was admired for its delicacy and sheen. Like the linen-thread laces of Lille, it was made with open grounds and light, geometric patterns.

The centre for the industry at this time was the region around Paris but other centres and, indeed, other countries made their own blondes. As lace designs generally grew lighter, blonde became ever more favoured and was even found suitable for trimming the neo-classical dress of the early 1800s.

By the 1810s and 1820s, its popularity had grown to such an extent that it was used for flounces, pelerines, stoles and veils and even for whole dresses. Here was the reaction against the earlier simplicity of dress; when everyone wore muslin, mistress and maid were indistinguishable but an overdress of silk lace was only for the wealthy.

In the early 1800s, Chantilly, a small town to the north of Paris, and Caen in Normandy produced the finest blondes but in the late 1820s their manufacture was taken up in Bayeux. Here Lefébure, a leading manufacturer of his day, developed the trade with Spain and the Spanish colonies by producing a more heavily-patterned blonde, suited to their taste. This became known as 'blonde matte' or 'Spanish blonde' and was made in the usual cream or white silk, but also in black.

In the late 1830s and 1840s black lace was also becoming popular in northern Europe but the taste for blonde was waning or being satisfied by machine-made copies. The French workers were adaptable; they turned their skills to the 'Chantilly' laces and their prosperity continued as we shall see in the next chapter.

In the later 19th century, blonde regained some favour, particularly in its black form, but Spain was its major consumer. It had its own blonde industry in Catalonia and continued to make shawls, mantillas and other articles, both for home use and for its colonies. Often these can be distinguished from the French products by their less regular workmanship, coarse thread and uneven colouring, often tending to brown rather than black with age.

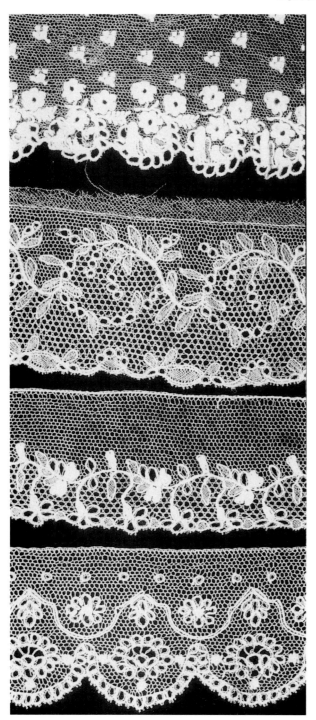

PLATE 150: **Group of blonde edgings.**

a. Early 19th C: 1820–30. (See Plate 149 for detail.)
  Depth 10 cm (4 in)
  Pattern repeat 3.5 cm (1.3 in)

b. Early–mid 19th C.
  Depth 9 cm (3.5 in)
  Pattern repeat 7.5 cm (3 in)
Both the point de Paris (kat stitch) and the Lille grounds are used
in this example. The pattern areas are in half stitch with a floss
silk used only for the gimp outline.

c. Early–mid 19th C.
  Depth 7 cm (2.8 in)
  Pattern repeat 5 cm (2 in)
Both the point de Paris and Lille grounds are again used.

d. Late 19th C: 1850–70.
  Depth 8.5 cm (3.4 in)
  Pattern repeat 6 cm (2.5 in)
Here the pattern is created almost entirely by the corded gimp
thread.

PLATE 151:

a. Black blonde shawl; probably Spanish: 2nd half of the 19th C.
  Depth shown 36 cm (14.5 in)
  Width shown 55 cm (21.5 in)
  Actual width 97 cm (38 in)
  Actual length 220 cm (86 in)
This stylized floral design is seen as early as the 1840s, but it
appears to have continued in use throughout the second half of the
19th century when it appealed particularly to the Spanish market.
The end strip is clearly worked in a different direction from the
strips which make up the main body of the shawl.

b. Black blonde shawl; probably Spanish: about 1880–1900.
  Depth shown 39 cm (15.5 in)
  Width shown 57 cm (22.5 in)
  Actual depth 70 cm (28 in)
  Actual length 200 cm (78 in)
The pretty but rather vapid floral motif is a common feature in
late 19th-century designs.

CHANTILLY

PLATE 152: Bonnet veil: about 1850–60.
Depth 47 cm (18.5 in)
Width 103 cm (41 in)

Characteristics

1. Straight bobbin lace, usually in dull black silk (grenadine) thread but sometimes in ivory.
2. Half stitch pattern areas.
3. Thick gimp outline to the pattern usually formed by a bundle of threads.
4. Splits often found in large pieces – these form along joins between pattern pieces. (The 'point de racroc' joining stitch is usually invisible to the naked eye.)
5. Grounds:

    a. Chantilly ground (kat stitch, point de Paris, Figure 27). Hexagonal mesh giving the appearance of a six-pointed star – the central hole is surrounded by six smaller holes each formed by a triangle of three pairs of threads.

    b. Fond simple (East Midlands point ground, Lille ground, Figure 28). Hexagonal mesh with four sides of two twisted threads and two sides of two threads crossed. This is more common in the second half of the 19th century.

Points to watch

Black East Midlands (Buckinghamshire) point laces are technically similar but sometimes distinguishable by their patterns or their thread.

Extremely close imitations of Chantilly lace were made on various machines (see page 183). The gimp thread is usually the clearest distinguishing feature: in some machine laces it is darned in by hand; in others it is incorporated by the machine but is caught on to the surface of the lace rather than within the thickness; in yet others it is incorporated by the machine but has cut ends at two places where it surrounds a motif, whereas a hand-made lace normally has cut ends at only one place.

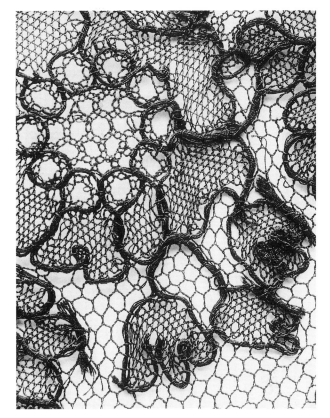

PLATE 153: **Detail of Plate 152 showing the half stitch pattern, the gimp outline, the fond simple ground, and a 'honeycomb' filling.**

History

We have already seen that Chantilly was a centre of the blonde-lace industry in the early 19th century and references to 'Chantilly' lace up till that time most probably relate to these shiny silk laces rather than to the lace we have

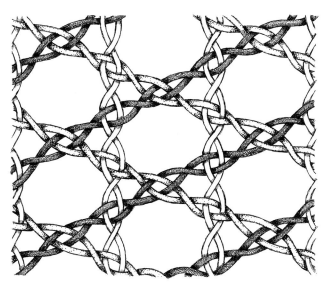

FIGURE 27: **Fond chant or kat stitch ground.**

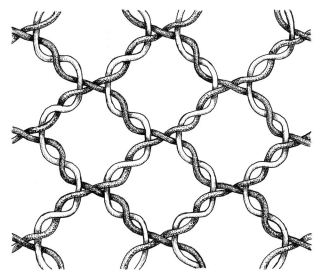

FIGURE 28: **Fond simple or Lille ground.**

come to associate with the name. It was not until the 1840s that tastes in northern Europe turned away from the cream laces and towards the black and the Chantilly manufacturers developed the use of the dull black silk thread known as grenadine. Had this been worked in the dense designs of the blonde laces, the name of Chantilly might never have been fêted across Europe. As it was, the working of naturalistic floral designs in the light texture of half stitch created a delicate fabric which displayed to dazzling effect over the pale or the richly coloured dresses of the period.

By the 1850s the manufacture of Chantilly lace had spread to Caen and Bayeux and even to Belgium but Chantilly still kept the reputation for the highest quality. By now every manner of dress accessory was made in this fabric, even to the huge flounces and shawls needed to cover the full skirts worn over the ever-expanding crinoline frame. Such large pieces could not, of course, be made in one piece by the straight bobbin technique and designs were split into smaller, manageable parts for working.

In the late 1850s and 1860s Chantilly was one of the

PLATE 154: **Shoulder cape of Chantilly lace: about 1860–75.**
  Depth of edging forming the neck frill 5 cm (2 in)
  Depth of central panel, excluding frill 33 cm (13 in)
The neck frill is a Chantilly-type edging but of poorer quality than the main body of the cape and is sewn to it. The cape itself is made in several panels, all carefully joined on the pillow by the 'point de racroc'. Straight splits are often found in Chantilly laces where the joins pass through the net; other joins are formed around outlines in a design.

favourite laces at the French court but the collapse of the Second Empire in 1870 and the accompanying changes in fashion brought about a drastic reduction in its market. Much lace from this period went into store, not to be sold until its return to fashion in the 1890s.

The production of this later period was often in slightly stiffer versions of the earlier designs, much of it in a coarser thread, but it never reached the volume of the earlier periods and little has been made this century.

b

c

a

PLATE 155:

a. (*right*). Lappet end: about 1870–90.
  Width 16 cm (6.3 in)
  Length shown 33 cm (13 in)
  Full length of single lappet 80 cm (31 in)
This is one end of a pair of lappets made in one piece in the 19th-century manner. The design is stiffer and more formal than those of the veil and cape in Plates 152 and 154 and suggests a later date.

b. (*upper left*). Edging: about 1890–1900.
  Depth 9 cm (3.5 in)
  Pattern repeat 9 cm (3.5 in)
The late date of this place is suggested by the weakness of the design, particularly of the opposing C-shaped scrolls.

c. (*lower left*). Edging: about 1855–75.
  Depth 12 cm (4.7 in)
I have classified this piece as a Chantilly because its thread, particularly the gimp outline, and its use of the fond simple ground in the central band are what one associates with Chantilly lace. Clearly its geometric design is utterly different from the floral designs one expects of Chantilly laces but during the lace boom of the 1850s and 1860s many styles of design coexisted and were transferred from one technique to another. As we shall see in the next few chapters, geometric-styled guipures were particularly popular during this period and copies in lighter laces were by no means uncommon.

MALTESE

PLATE 156: Maltese fascinator: second half of the 19th C;
probably 1850–75.
  Overall length (when flat) 145 cm (57 in)
  Depth of centre piece 59 cm (23 in)
The 'fascinator' is simply one name for this shaped head covering
with a wide centre piece which drapes over the head and lappets
which are long enough to be tied beneath the chin. Its large size
distinguishes it from the fall caps seen in Plates 41 and 147.

Fascinators can sometimes be confused with double fichu
collars (Plate 148), which have a similar shape when opened out,
but the fascinator will usually lie flat when spread whereas the
double collar is often shaped to curve around the shoulders and
will not lie flat.

This fascinator is carefully worked in a very fine, cream floss
silk which suggests a date in the middle of the 19th century. It is
worked in seven parts: the central cross; three concentric areas
around the cross; the scalloped border; and the two centres of the
lappets.

Characteristics

1. Straight bobbin lace, usually in floss silk thread – cream, black or ivory – but also in cotton.
2. Uniform threads – no thick gimp or raised work.
3. Clothwork pattern areas, usually including the Maltese cross.
4. Frequent use of fat wheatears with pointed ends, often grouped in star formations.
5. Splits often found where pattern pieces are coming apart due to breaks in the overcasting thread used to sew adjacent edges together.
6. Grounds:
   Varied arrangements of twisted and plaited brides combined with wheatears.

Points to watch

Maltese lace can be very difficult to date because its designs remained substantially unchanged throughout its history. Two factors can help: the style of the costume item which it forms and the quality of the thread and workmanship.

The Maltese cross is usually, but not invariably, found in the design. It was probably introduced in the 1850s, to distinguish true Maltese lace from the copies which proliferated throughout Europe as a result of its extraordinary rise in popularity. When the cross is absent, the presence of fat, pointed wheatears may indicate a Maltese origin.

History

It may be thought that the stylized floral and geometric designs of Maltese lace, and particularly the use of wheatears, are reminiscent of early 17th-century Italian laces. This is not just coincidence. In the 1830s Malta was suffering from famine and lace-makers from Genoa, where the old traditions survived, were introduced to pass on their skills. This charitable act is said to have been the work of Lady Hamilton Chichester, better known for her association with Admiral Lord Nelson.

The timing was apt. Fashionable taste was tending towards fuller designs and the display of Maltese lace at the Great Exhibition at Crystal Palace in 1851 excited the whole of Europe. The industry flourished; flounces, fichus, parasol covers and the huge triangular or square shawls worn over the wide crinolines of the 1860s were all made in this boldly patterned fabric.

In the 1870s, when many of the lace industries of Europe were suffering from competition with machine-made products, the Maltese industry was able to continue because of the popularity and comparative cheapness of its laces. These were, in any case, relatively quick to make but the standards of workmanship dropped and coarser threads were introduced.

The revival of interest in handicrafts in the 1890s and 1900s led to some better work being done. Laces from this period can often be distinguished by their thick, very lustrous thread which gives the proliferation of wheatears an

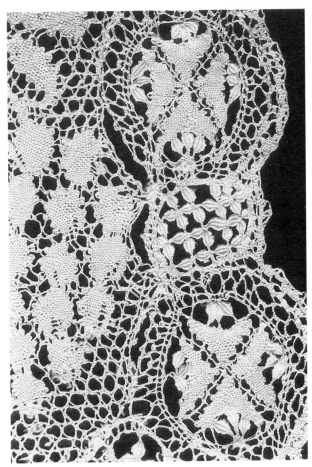

PLATE 157: Detail of the edge of one of the lappets in Plate 156.
Note the typical clothworked Maltese cross, pointed wheatears and the loosely-worked, open ground. The area of kat stitch on the left is much less common.
The gaps between the scalloped edge and the central part of the lappet are due to the breaking of the thread used to sew the two parts together.

almost three-dimensional appearance; laces of this type always remind me of modern bubble-pack wrapping.

Another innovation in the 1890s or 1900s was the introduction of a bleached white silk thread. Nearly all the earlier silk laces had been in cream or black and these colours continued to be used although black was considerably less popular in the 20th century.

The disappearance of lace from dress in the First World War marked the death of many of the lace industries of Europe. The Maltese industry survived, if on a much reduced scale, by supplying souvenirs to the British troops stationed on the island and to the tourist trade which followed. It was in the period between the two World Wars that much of the household lace, dressing table sets, place mats, etc, in white or ecru cotton, was made and imported into Britain with thousands of silk handkerchiefs with skimpy edgings barely recognizable as Maltese lace.

PLATE 158:

a.   Maltese flounce: second half of the 19th C; probably about 1850–75.

   Maximum depth 13 cm (52 in)

   Pattern repeat 7 cm (2.7 in)

The fine quality of this piece again suggests a date nearer the middle than the end of the 19th century. It is worked in a fine, lustrous, black silk thread.

b.   Maltese bonnet veil: about 1850–70.

   Maximum depth 43 cm (17 in)

   Maximum width 82 cm (32.2 in)

Semi-circular bonnet veils which draped closely round the face were popular with the smaller bonnets of the 1850s and 1860s.

   Note the Maltese crosses in the scalloped edge which are depicted in outline. Designs including narrow trails of clothwork instead of broad areas are common in black Maltese laces to give a lighter effect, especially when a cotton thread or dull silk is used as in this piece.

LE PUY

PLATE 159: Shawl or fichu collar: about 1860–80.
   Depth of lace at centre 40 cm (16 in)
   Width of neck opening 24 cm (9.5 in)
The design and work involved in this piece are poorer and less
skilled than in the flounces in Plate 160 but its large scale, the use
of patterned strapwork and the contrast given by different
densities of stitching are typical of Le Puy work.

History

Le Puy and the surrounding region of the Auvergne have a
long lacemaking tradition, stretching back at least to the
17th century. Then, and in the 18th century, the Auvergne
produced many of the simpler, cheaper types of lace,
including the blonde laces which become popular in the
second half of the 18th century. The region suffered greatly
from the decline at the turn of the 19th century and it was
not until the 1820s and 1830s, when various manufacturers
took the organization of the industry in hand, that the tide
turned. Workers were trained in more skilled techniques,
new designs were supplied and new ideas tried and tested.

One of the innovations of this period was a black silk
guipure lace which was closely followed by a white guipure
in imitation of the Maltese lace which was becoming
popular. These were the laces for which Le Puy was to
become famous: not that these were the only laces then made
in the area, nor that these guipures were made only at Le
Puy. Many lace-making areas of Europe took to copying the
Maltese laces more or less closely since they were quicker

and cheaper to make than the net-grounded laces and their bold designs were fasionable at the time.

A major advantage of the Le Puy region was that its more influential manufacturers had Parisian bases with access to the latest fashions and the best designers. Whereas the designs of Malta and other minor lace-making areas fossilized, the Le Puy workers had a constant supply of the most up-to-date patterns. These included formal designs of cartouches and fan shapes defined by patterned strapwork closely resembling that of the best Chantilly and Brussels laces. What was omitted in these guipure laces was the floral aspect of the more opulent designs, and even this was to some extent remedied by the introduction of panels of Chantilly-type lace.

In the 1860s a simpler version of the geometric Maltese lace was introduced; this was known as 'Cluny' lace (see pages 82–5) and was made alongside the better quality laces. With the fall of the French Second Empire in 1870 and the consequent depression in the French industry, the renowned adaptability of the Le Puy workers enabled them to maintain a certain degree of prosperity by turning to other types of lace, including torchon and simple guipures in cotton, wool and metal threads, much of it for export. This was sufficient to keep the industry alive until the First World War but there was little recovery afterwards and now the Le Puy shops are filled largely with machine-made lace.

PLATE 160: All three pieces in this plate date from the second half of the 19th century, probably from about 1860–80.

a. Edging in black silk.
    Depth 8 cm (3.7 in)
    Pattern repeat 6 cm (2.4 in)
I include this edging with the Le Puy laces since it has several characteristics typical of the so-called Le Puy type, i.e. a ground of large-scale meshes formed by picoted brides; long wheatears with pointed ends; and inserted panels of Chantilly-type lace. Narrow edgings of this type with comparatively simple designs were made in various areas of Europe; this may be an English piece.

b. Flounce.
    Depth 15.5 cm (6 in)
    Pattern repeat 10 cm (4 in)
The stylish design including a motif resembling a *fleur de lys* suggests a French origin for this piece. The complex ground in the upper part is typical of the Le Puy lace but there are no wheatears or areas of Chantilly lace; the simple Lille net ground is used as a filling in the elongate teardrop shapes, but is worked in the same thread as the rest of the lace.

c. Flounce.
    Depth 18.5 cm (7.2 in)
    Pattern repeat 9.5 cm (3.7 in)
This piece has all the characteristics of true Le Puy lace: complex ground, Chantilly-like panels, an organized design with strapwork and fan shapes patterned with rows of elongate wheatears, although these are not always well made nor with nicely pointed ends. More unusually, the Chantilly panels are decorated with wheatears worked over the surface (see Plate 161).

PLATE 161: **Detail of the flounce in Plate 160*c*.**

Characteristics

1. Straight bobbin lace, usually in black silk but also in blonde or white silk or in cotton.
2. Uniform threads except for insertions of Chantilly lace in finer thread.
3. Designs of small clothwork areas and trailing lines defining areas filled with other stitches, particularly fond simple and rows of long, narrow wheatears, usually with pointed ends.
4. Grounds:
    Various well-ordered arrangements of plaited and twisted brides forming large-scale, often complex meshes.

Points to watch

This is a derivative of Maltese lace (see pages 170–172) as is the related East Midlands (Bedfordshire) guipure (see pages 176–179). The simpler guipure laces made in England, Le Puy and elsewhere in Europe, are often indistinguishable from each other.

EAST MIDLANDS
(BEDFORDSHIRE) GUIPURE

Characteristics

1. Straight bobbin lace.
2. Clothwork pattern areas sometimes incorporating gimp threads within or outlining the design.
3. Frequent use of tallies (wheatears), most commonly with square ends, and areas of point ground (see Figure 25, page 155) as a filling.
4. Designs of trailing lines and simple leaf and flower shapes.
5. Ground:
   Irregular arrangements of plaited and twisted brides.

Points to watch

See Le Puy laces (pages 173–5) and bobbin laces in geometric designs (pages 82–5). The semi-straight technique was used for complex designs.

History

The name of Bedfordshire is now associated with the guipure lace just described but this was a comparatively recent introduction. In the 18th and early 19th centuries the English East Midlands counties had been involved in the making of straight laces with open net grounds and it was not until the 1840s that guipures started to return to fashion.

As we have seen in an earlier chapter (pages 154–61), by this time the making of point lace was in decline because of competition from machine laces and because of the renewed interest in more richly designed continental laces. Many of the English lace-makers turned to other forms of employment while others turned their talents to the guipure laces which were quicker and easier to make than the point lace.

Impetus for this change was given particularly by the success of the Maltese laces at the Great International Exhibition in 1851. This resulted in copies of the Maltese style which have come to be known as 'Bedfordshire Maltese' although they were, in fact, also made in the neighbouring counties of Buckinghamshire and Northamptonshire.

The general trend in the 1850s and 1860s was to increase the rate of production as the demand for lace increased but competition with the machine products forced prices down.

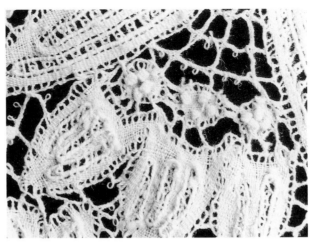

PLATE 163: Detail of the collar in Plate 162, showing the dense clothwork and picoted bar ground which are typical of East Midlands guipures. The use of a gimp thread is quite common but the very neat, raised tallies worked over the surface are particularly fine.

As in the Devon industry, the quality of design and workmanship declined: the earlier, more intricate patterns of stylized flowers and trailing clothwork set against complex grounds were largely replaced by the simpler 'Cluny' laces.

Only a few manufacturers held out. The firm of Thomas Lester in Bedford was noted for its efforts to provide good designs and to ensure a high standard of workmanship from its employees. Many of these designs with their naturalistically drawn flowers are similar to those of the Honiton guipures of the period. Their complexity necessitated the splitting of the design into small areas for working or the borrowing of techniques, such as the use of sewings to join touching edges, from the part laces.

A few manufacturers followed Thomas Lester's lead but the quantity of these higher-quality products was small compared with the mass of poorly-made lace. Like Devon, the Midlands suffered from the poor organization of the industry. Many of the middlemen who distributed lace patterns to the cottagers and later brought their lace for sale in the towns saw their workers once in a few weeks. They had no control over standards of workmanship nor over where the lace made on their patterns was sold. With pay so low that many could scarcely earn a living wage by working 14 hours a day no loyalty could be expected, nor was there any incentive to provide new, better and more expensive patterns.

With conditions as they were, it is surprising that the industry survived the recession of the 1870s, but as in other regions, there was a resurgence at the end of the century. Lace continued to be made commercially into this century though on a very reduced scale.

PLATE 162:
a. Corn motif: late 19th C.
   Depth 31 cm (12.3 in)

b. Collar: about 1870–90.
   Length of inside edge 87 cm (34.5 in)
   Maximum width 63 cm (25 in)
Both of these pieces are of good quality; the collar is exceptional. Designs of this complexity could not be worked purely by the straight technique and include sewings to join touching edgings. (See Plate 163 for detail.)

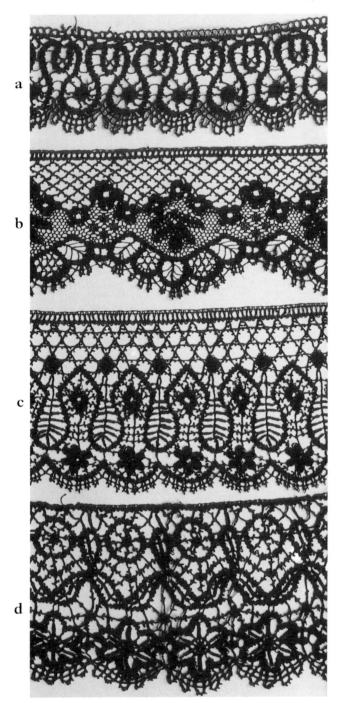

a

b

c

d

PLATE 164: Group of black East Midlands edgings from the second half of the 19th C.

Length shown 18 cm (7 in)

These are typical products of the East Midlands industry but could equally well have been made in Belgium, France or other lace-making areas of Europe. Examples *c* and *d* are of the type referred to as 'Bedfordshire Maltese' and probably date from the 1850s to 1870s. (*a*) and (*b*) are probably later.

a. Depth 5.5 cm (2.2 in); pattern repeat 3 cm (1.2 in)

b. Depth 8 cm (3.2 in); pattern repeat 9 cm (8.5 in)
Note the use of a coarse version of the Midlands point ground in addition to the picoted bar ground.

c. Depth 10 cm (4 in); pattern repeat 3.5 cm (1.4 in)

d. Depth 10.5 cm (4.2 in); pattern repeat 4.5 cm (1.8 in)

PLATE 165:
a. Collar: late 19th–20th C.
    Depth of lace 7.5 cm (3 in)
    Length of inner edge 34 cm (13.5 in)
Designs including this simple flowerhead with its point ground centre, the pointed leaf and the edging of tiny, picoted scallops, called a '9-pin edging', were in use for at least 50 years.

b. Fragment of an edging: 2nd half of the 19th C.
    Depth 6.5 cm (2.6 in)
    Pattern repeat 3.5 cm (1.4 in)
This is worked in a finer thread than examples *a*, *c*, and *d* and is probably of earlier date.

c. Edging: 2nd half of the 19th C.
    Depth 6 cm (2.4 in)
    Pattern repeat 4 cm (1.6 in)
This has a ground of tallies arranged to form square meshes, known as 'plaited ground'.

d. Cuff: about 1870–90.
    Width 27 cm (10.7 in)
    Depth 12 cm (4.8 in)

a

b

c

d

SUMMARY OF THE MOST COMMON HAND-MADE NET GROUNDS

COLLATED here are only those grounds commonly associated with specific types of lace. Other grounds were used in the major lace types and the features listed in the foregoing chapters must be used in association with the grounds before a lace can be identified.

Brussels point de gaze
Rows of buttonhole stitches each looped into a stitch in a previous row to form fine meshes, usually about 1 mm across and roughly hexagonal to the naked eye. Found mainly in Brussels laces from the mid-19th to the 20th centuries, in needlepoint, bobbin, or mixed bobbin and needlepoint laces.

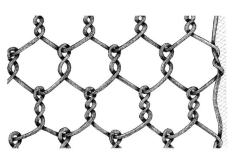

Alençon
Rows of buttonhole stitches as above but with each row strengthened by an additional thread run back through the stitches. In good-quality, unrepaired work the meshes are roughly hexagonal to the naked eye and about $\frac{1}{2}$ mm to 1 mm across but repairs often pull the meshes into rectangles. Found in French needlepoints from the mid-18th to 20th centuries, in 19th-century Honiton and Brussels bobbin laces and in tape laces.

Burano
Rows of buttonhole stitches strengthened with an additional thread but this is pulled taut and distorts the meshes into rectangles about $\frac{1}{2}$ mm to 1 mm across, giving a ladder-like appearance. Found in Burano laces of the 18th century and late 19th to 20th century and in repaired Alençon laces.

Argentan
Coarse hexagonal meshes about 2 mm across with closely worked buttonhole stitches along each side. Found in French needlepoints from the early 18th century onwards but rare after 1780.

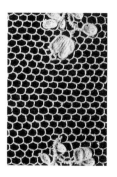

PLATE 166: **Argentan ground.**

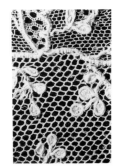

Tortillée

Hexagonal meshes with each side strengthened with widely spaced buttonhole stitches or a twisted thread: mesh size about 1 mm. Found in French needlepoints from the late 18th century.

PLATE 167: **Tortillée ground.**

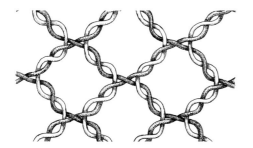

Fond simple or point ground

Meshes formed with four sides of two twisted threads and two sides of two threads crossed, and appearing hexagonal to the naked eye. Found in Lille, East Midlands (Bucks) point, Chantilly, blonde, Tønder (Danish) and other bobbin laces from the late 18th century onwards. Many machine nets also have this form.

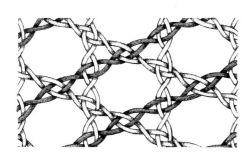

Kat stitch (or fond chant, Chantilly, point de Paris, wire ground)

Meshes appearing like six pointed stars with a central hexagon surrounded by six triangles. Found in Chantilly, East Midlands (Bucks) point, blonde and other bobbin laces from the mid-17th century onwards. There are many slight variations on the stitch shown.

Flemish round ground

This ground has several common variations but, in general, has hexagonal meshes with four threads plaited or crossed on all six sides. Mesh size – several mm. Found in Flemish and North Italian laces from the mid-17th century onwards, the Italian ground usually being more tightly worked. Eighteenth century Flemish part laces are usually grounded with a much more open variation.

A fine version with a mesh size of about 1 mm is found in 18th-century Valenciennes laces.

Valenciennes carrée, or diamond ground

Diamond-shaped mesh with four threads plaited on each side. The length of the sides varies considerably from about 1 mm to 3 mm. Introduced into Valenciennes laces in the late 18th century and typical in the 19th century.

Mechlin 'Eis' ground

Regular hexagonal meshes with four sides of two twisted or crossed threads and two sides of four plaited threads but shorter than Vrai Drochel. Found in Mechlin laces from about the 1730s onwards.

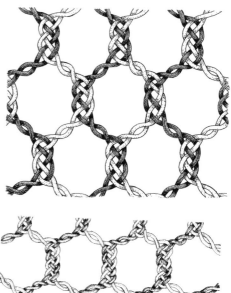

Brussels Vrai Drochel

Slightly elongate hexagonal meshes formed with four sides of two twisted threads and two sides of four plaited threads. Found in Brussels and Devon (Honiton) bobbin lace and as a ground for Brussels needlepoints from the early 18th century to the mid-19th century.

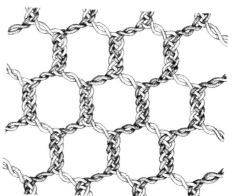

MACHINE v. HAND-MADE

Since the first machine-made nets were produced over 200 years ago, enormous quantities of lace have been produced on a wide variety of machines. Here are just a few examples to indicate some features to look for when sorting hand- from machine-made lace.

PLATE 168:

a. (*left*). Burano needlepoint.

b. Machine imitation of a needlepoint.

Early machine laces imitated hand laces as closely as possible. Although imitations improved generally in the 19th century, any one machine might be used to imitate various hand laces, with greater or lesser success. Here the well-defined raised outline on the right side of the lace suggests a needlepoint cordonnet but the ribbed appearance of the clothwork is totally different from the buttonholed clothwork of the needlepoint. No machine has ever successfully imitated the looped structure of needlepoint laces, and, in particular, the closely button-holed bars and cordonnets of some needlepoints.

This type of machine lace often imitates Mechlin laces but, in a straight bobbin lace, the gimp thread is incorporated within the thickness of the lace and is seen on both sides: it does not lie on one side as in this machine example.

PLATE 169: Machine imitation of a 19th-C bobbin guipure.

This very effective imitation includes many features of the original: trails of clothwork; wheatears; a complex but regular ground of picoted bars; etc. The only immediate indication of its machine origin is the ribbed appearance of the clothwork: in contrast, note the even texture of the clothwork in Plates 160–165. Close inspection of the grounds and edging also reveals a complex, twisted structure in which it is impossible to follow individual threads. To the naked eye this appears solely as a slight fuzziness but this and the ribbed clothwork are common features of machine laces.

PLATE 170:
a. (*left*). Machine imitation of an East Midlands bobbin lace.
b. Machine imitation of Mechlin lace.

a. The kat-stitch ground, cloth-stitch pattern and filling stitches, are, at first glance, typical of an East Midlands lace but the gimp thread passes in and out of the lace: it was not caught between the working threads as the lace was made but was run in by hand with a needle afterwards. When magnified, the lace structure is also seen to be confused.

b. The gimp is again the give-away here. It is caught between the threads of the lace but has cut ends at both ends of pattern areas which it surrounds: in a hand-made bobbin lace the gimp is cut at only one end of a motif.

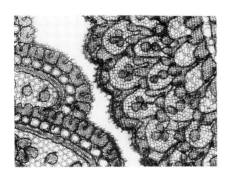

PLATE 171:
a. (*left*). Hand-made Chantilly lace.

b. (*right*). Machine imitation of Chantilly lace.

b. This clever imitation has the half stitch pattern, point ground and multi-stranded gimp of the Chantilly. The gimp even surrounds the pattern areas with few breaks but, in fact, it passes in and out of the lace – it is hand-run like the gimp in Plate 170a.

Another clue to the machine origin is the stretched appearance of the half-stitch pattern – the hand-made half stitch is far more open and regular in appearance.

In other close imitations of Chantilly, the gimp is incorporated in the fabric by the machine but has cut ends at each end of a motif as in Plate 170*b*.

PLATE 172:
a. and c.   Machine imitations of 19th-C Valenciennes laces.

b.   Hand-made 19th-C Valenciennes lace.

a. This completely flat lace with its diamond-shaped ground immediately suggests a 19th-century Valenciennes lace but the ribbed clothwork indicates its machine origin. Close inspection of the ground also shows a confused, twisted structure, not the neat plaits of the hand-made lace.

c. This is a much more convincing imitation than *a*. The clothwork is of varying density as in the hand-made example and only the spots are slightly ribbed. The ground has round meshes but these are sometimes found in the hand-made lace (see Plate 127*b*): only close inspection shows that the ground has a confused rather than a neatly plaited structure.

PLATE 173: Two examples of chemical lace:

a. (*left*). Imitation of Irish crochet in the style of late 17th C Venetian needlepoints.

b. (*right*). Imitation mid-17th C Venetian rose point (Plate 18). (A further example is shown in Plate 108.)

'Chemical' lace is a machine embroidery which was developed in the 1880s. It derives its name from the fact that the embroidery is carried out on a fabric which is subsequently dissolved chemically to leave the lace-like textiles. The technique has been used particularly to imitate guipure needlepoints but can also produce fine meshes or can be worked on a machine-made net to imitate mesh-grounded laces.

Although used here to imitate needlepoint or crochet, close inspection shows no chain stitch or buttonhole stitches; instead, the clothwork looks like needleweaving and the ground is very confused and fuzzy.

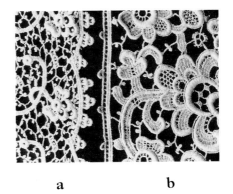

a   b

HOW TO IDENTIFY – SOME WORKED EXAMPLES

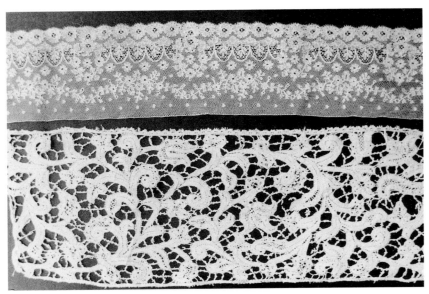

a

b

PLATE 174:
a.   Edging:
   Depth 10 cm (4 in); pattern repeat 11.5 cm (4.5 in)

b.   Flounce:
   Depth 15 cm (6 in); pattern repeat – more than 32 cm (13 in)
(design cut and reversed at a later date).

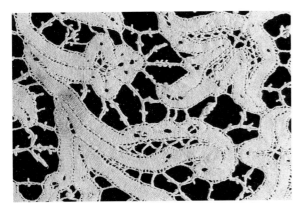

PLATE 175: **Detail of Plate 174*b*.**

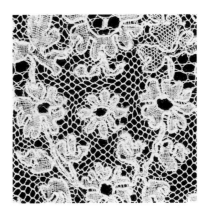

PLATE 176: **Detail of Plate 174*a*.**

IN this book we have used close-up photographs to enable the reader to see the fine structure of a lace which enables its type to be determined. To study actual examples, the reader must procure a strong magnifying glass. In many cases, 10 × magnification will suffice, but 20 × magnification will sometimes be useful.

HERE five pieces of lace are examined to determine their type, their date, and if possible their place of origin; they have not been illustrated elsewhere.

Example 1 (PLATES 174*a* AND 176)

1 How was it made – with bobbins, a needle, . . . ?

Looking for obvious features we see a pattern including woven clothwork: this suggests a bobbin lace. Looking more closely we see that the threads of the net ground continue into the pattern, suggesting a bobbin-made straight lace, but this feature also occurs in some machine laces.

The clothwork is unridged, the path of the threads in the net is clear and there is a gimp thread which is caught between pairs of the finer threads and cut at only one end of the motifs it surrounds. This is a true BOBBIN lace.

2 What type of lace is it?

It has a net ground – is it illustrated on pages 180–2?

The fine hexagonal meshes have two thicker sides which may be plaited: this is confirmed under strong magnification. This may be the Mechlin eis ground or the vrai drochel used in Brussels and Honiton laces. In the respective chapters we find that the straight technique and gimp thread are characteristic of MECHLIN laces: the Brussels and Honiton are both part laces.

3 Date and Origin?

Looking at the Mechlin chapter we see no design similar to Example 1, but what of the Alençon lace in Plate 31*a*? This has a similarly compartmented design along the headside and a trailing floral design nearer the footside; it dates from about 1850–75.

We also learn from the Mechlin chapter that the half stitch seen in Example 1 was introduced into Mechlin patterns in the later 19th century. This tends to confirm the date.

In the 19th century, particularly, not all Mechlin laces were made in Mechlin but the fine quality of this example suggests it is the product of a highly organized industry, such as that of Belgium.

4 *CONCLUSION*

A Mechlin-type lace of about 1850–75, probably Belgian.

Example 2 (PLATES 174*b* AND 175)

1 How was it made?

The pattern of woven clothwork again indicates a BOBBIN lace. This is confirmed by plaited brides linked into the edges of the pattern, unridged clothwork with threads smoothly following its twists and turns, and variations in its width and fillings – it is neither completely machine-made nor worked with a machine-made tape.

2 What type?

The threads of the bar ground do not continue into the pattern. This is a part or semi-straight guipure. Breaks in the design show it to be a part lace.

To identify a guipure we can start with the early bobbin chapters. We can rule out the geometric laces; but look at the Milanese work. On checking characteristics we find similarities – a part or semi-straight lace; a flowing baroque design formed by a varied tape with no gimp or raised work. 'Points to watch', however, directs us to Flemish laces (pages 92–103) and here we find similar characteristics. So: is it Italian or Flemish?

Looking more carefully at the ground we find many double brides. These meet in a manner not shown in the Milanese laces but there are similarities with Venetian needlepoints: a North Italian origin is suggested.

3 Date?

We can look at the designs in the Milanese and Flemish chapters and in the needlepoints. The flow and scale of the motifs are perhaps closest to those of the Flemish lace in Plate 85*a*, but the Flemish lace has a net ground. A quick check confirms that net and bar grounds co-existed, so 1670–90 is also possible for this example.

Before a positive conclusion is reached, however, could it be a later copy? Here only experience can help. The whole feel of the piece, its thread, its design, its technique, are right for a 17th-century lace.

4 *CONCLUSION*

A bobbin lace in the Italianate baroque style: probably North Italian, about 1670–90.

PLATE 177:

a. Edging:
Depth 9.5 cm (3.5 in); pattern repeat 16.5 cm (6.5 in)

b. Edging:
Depth 8 cm (3.3 in); pattern repeat 42 cm (16.5 in)

c. Edging:
Depth 13 cm (5 in); pattern repeat 15 cm (6 in)

PLATE 178:
a. **Detail of Plate 177b.**
b. **Detail of Plate 177c.**

Example 3 (PLATES 177*a* AND 179)

1 How was it made?

The obvious features are the tightly buttonholed bars and raised work. This is apparently a NEEDLEPOINT lace but one must check to eliminate the chain stitches of crochet.

2 What type?

This is a guipure so we must refer to the early needlepoint chapters. It does not have the simple, symmetrical designs of reticella and punto in aria but a flowing, Italian baroque style. This, and the elaborate surface work, suggest a Venetian rose point.

3 Date?

The design is of a similar scale to that of Example 3 but it does not have the same vigour. The flowing lines of the stems are broken by flowers and leaves which curl back over them. The filling stitches are far more open, the thread and texture of the work far coarser than one would expect of a 17th-century Venetian work.

4 CONCLUSION

This is one of the later copies of a late 17th-century Venetian needlepoint lace. It may have been made in Burano, Brussels, or elsewhere in about 1900.

Example 4 (PLATES 177*b* AND 178*a*)

1 How was it made?

The close buttonholing of the raised outline again immediately indicates a NEEDLEPOINT lace. This is confirmed by close inspection of the ground and pattern.

2 What type?

The net ground has fine meshes with two threads twisted on each side; this is the French Alençon or the Burano ground. The hexagonal shape suggests ALENÇON and if we check the characteristics of French and Burano needlepoints we find that the FRENCH needlepoints have the buttonholed outline.

3 Date?

A search for a closely similar design in this book is fruitless but we do note that sparse designs were popular from the 1760s to 1840s. This example does not have the simple, repetitive design of about 1800; the freedom of drawing of its sprigs and its scattering of insects are closer to the styles of Plates 96*c* and 134*c* than of Plate 30*d* or 135*a* and *b*.

4 CONCLUSION

A French needlepoint with the Alençon ground, of about 1770–85, from the Alençon/Argentan region of Normandy.

Example 5 (PLATES 177*c* AND 178*b*)

1 How was it made?

Pattern areas of woven clothwork indicate a bobbin lace but a closer look at the more open areas shows the looped structures of a needlepoint lace. The raised outlines also differ and a look at the back shows that the motifs are applied to the net ground. This is a MIXED lace.

2 What type?

Only one place is famous for mixed laces – BRUSSELS. Comparisons of the structure of the bobbin work and of the needlework with the Brussels chapters confirm this probability but what of the net ground? This is neither the Brussels point de gaze nor the vrai drochel but a simple twist net – its uniformity suggests machine manufacture.

3 Date and origin?

The twist net says '19th century'. The strapwork and ribbons in the design suggest post-1840 and fairly similar designs are seen in Plates 30*e* and 101*e*. The text indicates that manufacture tended to be outside Brussels at this time.

4 CONCLUSION

A Brussels mixed lace applied to a machine net: about 1850–75; probably Belgian, possibly Brussels work.

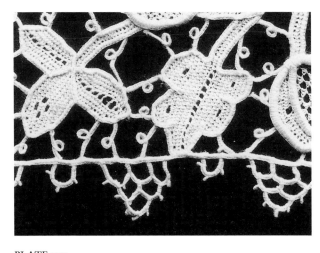

PLATE 179:
Detail of Plate 177*a*.

CLEANING, CARE AND CONSERVATION

WE are all used to handling fabrics in our everyday lives but expect to replace old clothes and furnishings after a limited lifetime. Lace, on the other hand, may already be over a hundred years old and much of it can never be replaced. It needs special treatment to preserve it for our own enjoyment and for future generations.

A detailed study of methods of conservation is beyond the scope of this book but I hope the following indication of dangers to avoid and the guide to washing and display will be of some help. For guidance on specific problems the reader should consult a book on textile conservation or a textile conservator.

Dangers

Air Air contains oxygen which reacts with the fibres in the lace in a very slow 'burning', or ageing, process. This is what causes white or cream laces to turn yellow. Washing will remove the yellow colour but weakens the lace since it removes the yellowed outer layers of the fibres, leaving the underlying fibres exposed.

Chemicals Acids and alkalis eat into textile fibres and, if they are left in the lace, it will eventually fall apart. Bleaches are the most common source of acids in lace but many chemicals, from modern biological detergents to grandmother's special recipe, are potentially harmful.

Creases Textile fibres break along creases if these are left for any length of time.

Cutting and rearranging This destroys the aesthetic quality and historical value of a lace, whether a complete article or a flounce. It is often unnecessary, may not have the desired effect of producing a usable item and reduces its financial value.

Dirt Dirt includes chemicals (see above) and also rough particles which abrade the fibres to break down their structure.

Handling This includes thoughtless handling by those unused to dealing with old fabrics who pull a collar into shape or stroke firmly to get its 'feel' not realizing that the tension created, if not actually tearing the lace apart, is stretching some fibres, breaking others and generally weakening the lace. What is less often realized is that even gentle handling is harmful. The SWEAT transferred to the lace is acidic (see 'Chemicals', above).

Heat and light Heat and light, particularly ultraviolet light, accelerate chemical reactions and quicken the degradation these cause.

Mending A bad mend can do more harm than good. Needles and pins pushed through the lace fibres can break them. Threads used to catch torn edges together or to darn holes can pull even larger holes in a fragile fabric. It is often safer and less unsightly to ignore tears and holes.

If you still think mending might help, a book on textile conservation or your local textile conservator may suggest the best thread and methods to use.

Washing Even washing can be harmful. The removal of yellow colouring has already been mentioned (see 'Air', above). The movement and handling of the lace during washing are obvious dangers; but there is yet another problem. Lace is usually composed of natural fibres which absorb water and swell when wet; this swelling can shatter old fibres and the lace may disintegrate. Chemicals in the lace may dissolve as acids and fragile laces, particularly silks, may disintegrate.

Treatment
Washing
a. If lace has to be washed to remove dirt, then use a large, clean, shallow container with a plastic sheet in the bottom on which the lace can be spread as flat as possible.
b. Always remove the lace from the container by

means of the sheet which thus supports its weight, especially when wet.

c.   Use distilled or de-ionized water, if possible throughout the process but at least for the last one or two rinses.

d.   Soak the lace in cold water before washing to loosen dirt and stains.

e.   Use cold or lukewarm water for washing and cold water for rinsing.

f.   For washing, use a dilute solution of a mild liquid detergent such as Stergene (Reg'd T.M.). Allow the lace to soak in the solution for an hour. Brush discoloured areas very gently or force liquid through by gentle pressure with a sponge. **Do not rub!**

g.   After washing rinse at least three times until there is no more sign of the detergent. For stubborn stains the washing may be repeated. Stains are often preferable to the holes left by bleaches and stain-removers but, if you should use them, remember it is safer to use very dilute solutions repeatedly than to use a strong solution. Wash and rinse *very* thoroughly afterwards.

NOTE.   Stains are often less noticeable when the lace is dry.

Drying

a.   Lift the lace, right side uppermost, out of its last rinsing water on the plastic sheet and place on a flat surface.

b.   Add distilled water if necessary and gently float the lace out to its proper shape.

c.   Soak up excess water with clean white fabric and leave to dry.

Ironing   Avoid whenever possible; but if necessary, use a cool setting and iron raised laces upside-down on a towel. Gentle steaming with distilled water is often sufficient to remove creases.

Storage   Lace should be stored in cool, dry conditions, as flat as possible between layers of acid-free tissue paper. This is available from stationers: white is preferable as colours may run from coloured papers. If lace has to be folded, a roll of acid-free tissue paper in each fold will help prevent hard creases.

Flounces and edgings are best rolled on cardboard tubes, slightly longer than the width of the lace and covered with acid-free tissue, with tissue interleaved with the lace on the roll.

Display   Lace should be sewn on to a washed fabric supported on an acid-free backing. The backing should preferably be inclined rather than vertical to support the lace better. Lighting should be dim and/or the lace should be kept covered most of the time. The lace should not be in contact with glass or plastic.

READING LIST

BUCK, A., *Thomas Lester, his Lace and the East Midlands Industry 1820–1905*, Ruth Bean, 1981

CHANNER, C. C. and ROBERTS, M. E., *Lacemaking in the East Midlands*, Luton

EARNSHAW, P., *The Identification of Lace*, Shire, 1980

EARNSHAW, P., *Lace Machines and Machine Laces*, Batsford, 1986

FREEMAN, C., *Pillow Lace of the East Midlands*, Luton, 1958

HUDSON MOORE, N., *The Lace Book*, Chapman and Hall, 1905

INDER, P. M., *Honiton Lace*, Exeter

JOURDAIN, M., *Old Lace*, Batsford, 1908.

LEVEY, S. M., *Lace, A History*, Victoria and Albert Museum/Maney & Son, 1983.

LEVEY, S. M. & PAYNE, P. C., *Le Pompe, 1559: Patterns for Venetian Bobbin Lace*, Ruth Bean

LONGFIELD, A., *Irish Lace*, Eason & Son, Dublin

NEVILL JACKSON, F., *A History of Hand-made Lace*, Dover

PALLISER, BURY, *A History of Lace*, Dover, 1984

POLLEN, J. HUNGERFORD, *Seven Centuries of Lace*, Heinemann & Macmillan, 1908

SHARP, MARY, *Point and Pillow Lace*, John Murray, 1913

SIMEON, M., *The History of Lace*, Stainer & Bell, 1979

TOMLINSON, M., *Three Generations in the Honiton Lace Trade*, Devon Print Group

TREADWIN, MRS, *Antique Point Honiton Lace*

VINCIOLO, FREDERICO, *Renaissance Patterns for Lace, Embroidery and Needlepoint*, Dover

VON HENNEBERG, F. A., *The Art and Craft of Old Lace*, Batsford, 1931

VOYSEY, C., *Needlelace in Photographs*, Batsford, 1987

VOYSEY, C., *Bobbin lace in Photographs*, Batsford, 1987

WARDLE, P., *Victorian Lace*, Ruth Bean, 1982

WRIGHT, THOMAS, *The Romance of the Lace Pillow*, Minet Chicheley, 1971

YEFIMOVA, L. & BELOGORSKAYA, R., *Russian Embroidery and Lace*, Thames and Hudson

INDEX